# TEACHING
# WITH HEART

# TEACHING WITH HEART

*Lessons Learned in a Classroom*

## JENNIFER NELSON

SHE WRITES PRESS

Published 2023
Printed in the United States of America
Print ISBN: 978-1-64742-505-0
E-ISBN: 978-1-64742-505-0
Library of Congress Control Number: [LOCCN]

For information, address:
She Writes Press
1569 Solano Ave #546
Berkeley, CA 94707

*Interior design by Stacey Aaronson*
*Chapter illustrations by Shams Nelson*

She Writes Press is a division of SparkPoint Studio, LLC.

Teaching
with
Heart

# TABLE OF CONTENTS

# Prologue

I never thought I could be a high school teacher.

The best teachers ought to be patient, strict, and authoritative; I wasn't. They should adore teenagers. I wasn't sure I even liked them, perceiving them as moody and unpredictable. Besides, in the classroom, doesn't teaching the same material year after year get boring? Instead, I pictured myself in a profession working with adults, who were more interesting, relatable, much more likeable.

For years I worked as a journalist, writing stories for magazines and newspapers. Every day I learned something new, interviewing sources to discover what made them tick. I thrived in the newsroom, surrounded by irreverent, curious people. I had found my calling.

But circumstances changed. I divorced. The workload at the business journal burgeoned, and I felt I was neglecting my three young children at home. I'd always respected teachers, my family coming from a long line of educators. After much deliberation and some trepidation, I waded into teaching.

Could I transform myself into a model teacher? Did I have the personality to stand in front of aloof teenagers and engage them in French lessons? How did one do that? I had little formal training in education, but I was fluent in French. I would draw on my experience with the Peace Corps in Niger, where without textbooks or technology, I taught English to middle school French-speaking students.

Would I succeed? It wasn't clear how I would fare at private, public, and parochial schools, yet along the way, I picked up invaluable lessons. I learned how to control unruly teenagers and get them excited about learning even if they preferred playing video games and texting friends. I mastered the art of teaching millennials and Gen Z, disciplining teenagers, and communicating effectively with parents. Eventually, I realized why more than 50% of teachers want to leave the profession. I brainstormed ways to encourage teachers to stay in their profession.

This book provides advice on how veteran teachers can regain their sparkle, what to do the first days of school, and how to earn tenure.

I hope you benefit from my insights, regardless of whether you're new or experienced at teaching, a parent itching to know what's going on in classrooms, or a college student contemplating become a teacher. Our nation needs more people to enter this profession, and certainly with changes, more people will be attracted to the rewards and challenges of educating our youth.

## Chapter One

# THE DIRTY DOZEN

I t had been a horrible first few weeks at Northern High
School. My French 2 students were disengaged in lessons
that had worked well at the Catholic school where I'd previously
taught. They chatted, texted their friends, and copied homework—anything to avoid learning. But I hadn't given up. The nuns
had warned me about public school students; I'd have to create
gripping lessons for students to love French class—and me.

That Monday afternoon in late September, I smiled as I entered the gray classroom. I was confident Meghan, Danielle, and
Michael—the worst of the dozen—would treat me with respect

after that day's lesson. Certainly, they would be entertained by a PowerPoint presentation with alarms ringing, showers blasting, and buses whizzing. I had to turn this class around quickly; otherwise, I'd be fired or quit in desperation.

I spotted Michael, a tenth grader, sitting in back, his head resting on his desk.

"Bonjour Michel," I said, approaching him. He lay dormant. I tensed up, fearing his discontent if I woke him. At 1:20 p.m., the last period of the day, everyone was exhausted.

"Michel, *il faut te réveiller*," I said, nudging his shoulder.

His eyes flickered open. "Man, stop that," he said, nastily. "Don't touch me. That's sexual harassment. Get away from me."

*Really? He perceived a slight touch as sexual.*

I withdrew my arm as if I had just touched flames. I needed to reach him in a manner he found appropriate—my PowerPoint might be the answer.

"Michel, *on travail maintenant*," I said.

"I told you I don't know any French," he said, annoyingly. "We didn't learn shit last year. The teacher sucked."

*Profanity? Really? Girls at the Catholic school didn't swear. Should I write him up for a discipline referral? Tell him to stop? Or ignore it? What were the norms at this school?*

"I'm sure you learned something in French 1," I said reassuringly.

"Are you kidding?" said Michael. "All Mademoiselle talked about was her boyfriend."

Just then, the sound of boisterous voices broadcast Amanda and Meghan's entrance. "Madame, don't mark us late," said Amanda, a dark-haired beauty.

Everyone gazed as the drama queens marched into the classroom, its walls spotted with holes and dried-up tape. No teacher had beautified the classroom with posters; since I taught there only one period, I deferred to the main teacher to decorate it.

"One Monday morning, Mademoiselle came to class super tired," said Meghan, a cheerleader. "She told us she hadn't slept much because she had been making out all weekend with her boyfriend in San Francisco. She just gave us a handout to work on the whole period. Then she sat at her desk doing nothing. She was useless."

*Why would an adult ever talk to teenagers about her sex life? Some matters should remain private at school. No wonder her contract hadn't been renewed.*

"She wore super tight mini-skirts and tops," said Amanda, pushing her desk closer to Meghan's. "Her boobs hung out everywhere."

"The middle school principal loved watching her walk down the halls," blurted out Sara.

A few students giggled. I saw her as unprofessional, her dismissal no laughing matter.

"What are we doing today?" asked Amanda, doodling. "Probably nothing interesting."

*Wow, that hurt. Had these students been this obnoxious to Mademoiselle Bouvier? Is that why she prioritized her private life? Maybe I should do that with my own three children.*

"*J'ai préparé un* PowerPoint," I said.

Meghan's face glimmered with hope. "What about a PowerPoint? Are we doing one?"

*This was a good beginning; at least one person was intrigued by my lesson.*

"It's about daily routine," I answered. "Remember, we started this unit Friday?"

Three days earlier, students had listed words associated with daily hygiene—in English. Only Stephanie had written words in

French; I'd been amazed until she admitted her Senegalese parents spoke French at home. By Monday, students had forgotten the previous week's work.

Students drifted into class. Aravind reluctantly sat next to Michael, initiating a conversation with the only other boy in class. Michael remained taciturn. Elizabeth arrived, clutching her books to her chest as if blocking entry into her heart; she had recently moved from Arizona. As the bell rang, three freshmen, Sara, Chloe, and Danielle, rushed into the room.

The bell always signaled the start of class—and the end of talk about teachers' romantic escapades or anything besides French. To grab their attention, I projected the PowerPoint on the screen; it illuminated the room.

"*Regardez le* PowerPoint," I ordered.

I pointed at a slide of a teenager waking up, his hair disheveled, his room a mess.

Meghan and Amanda continued gossiping, Michael snoozed, and Elizabeth and two friends compared math homework. Only Aravind and Melissa gazed at the projector screen. At the time, PowerPoints were all the rage in education, a novelty guaranteed to engage students.

"*On commence la leçon,*" I said sternly. "*Mettez les devoirs de maths sous le pupitre.*'

Meghan and Amanda became silent. Michael raised his head. Elizabeth shoved her homework under the desk. They followed directions, understanding a little French. Success!

"That kid is like my buddy," said Aravind enthusiastically. "He doesn't comb his hair and clean his room."

"My mother would kill me if I left my room like that," said Meghan, her blond hair neatly tied back in a ponytail. "She always nags me about cleaning up. She needs to get a life."

Michael stared at the PowerPoint. "Man, that looks like a nice house."

He was living with a foster family after his father had hit him. My heart ached for him. I hoped, in class, I could help him forget his troubles at home.

"*Prenez un crayon et une feuille de papier,*" I said, holding up a pencil and paper. "*Prenez des notes sur le* PowerPoint."

Blank faces stared at me as if I had asked them to sing "La Marseillaise." Should I explain everything in English or continue to confuse them in French? I'd been trained to give the most important instructions in the target language, so that students would be motivated to understand information when the stakes were high—a quiz, a test, a big assignment. Also, students mastered French quicker if they heard only French. Yet, these teenagers didn't understand simple commands. Maybe I should ease them into immersion.

"Take notes on the PowerPoint," I said. "On paper, write down words on daily routine."

A cacophony of voices bombarded me: That was way too much work! No other teacher had forced them to take notes! Wasn't there a handout on the vocabulary? I explained they'd retain French words if they wrote them down.

*Wow, they're so lazy! What will make them work?*

Stephanie majestically walked into the room. I glanced at my watch—she was six minutes late. "I had to talk to my history teacher," she said. "I didn't understand an assignment."

"*Il faut être à l'heure,*" I said. "*Tu as un passe?*"

"Why do I need a pass?" she said rudely. "You trust me, don't you?"

During training, the district emphasized that students' social and emotional health was as important as their academic progress.

Didn't that mean I could ignore student tardiness? Wouldn't students feel anxious if they accumulated too many lates on their record?

"*Asseids-toi!*" I ordered Stephanie to sit down. "*Regardez la présentation sur la routine quotidienne. Prenez des notes.*"

"Sure," she answered, taking out a pen and paper.

Thank goodness, one student understood me. But if they'd had a competent teacher last year, most of them would have gotten the gist of my conversation.

For the first ten slides, students scribbled on paper. Yay! At last, they were working.

Yet, when they saw slides about life at school—meeting friends, studying, and eating lunch—they stopped writing. In English, they voiced their critiques: Kids in the presentation were too serious; they never had fun; their school was nicer than Northern. It went on and on. I had lost them. They hadn't penned a word of French for fifteen minutes.

If I'd been a savvy teacher, I might have announced their notes were worth points, enticing them to continue the task. Instead, I wallowed in self-pity, believing they should work quietly and diligently, no matter what they thought of the assignment. They criticized the presentation that had taken me hours to create. It was far more entertaining than the lessons I'd had as a teenager decades earlier, before technology changed the way students learned. How could I, a middle-aged woman who'd not used a computer until after college, relate to twenty-first century students hooked on cell phones, the Internet, and video games?

*Damn it, why did I work so hard for a lesson that was, again, a flop?*

★ ★ ★

The next day in the faculty room I approached Nabila, the school's veteran French teacher, who had befriended me over conversations about growing up abroad.

"Yesterday was a disaster," I said. "The kids didn't work. And I showed them an entertaining PowerPoint I made."

"I've had bad days; every teacher does," said Nabila, pushing aside the notebook she was grading. "The key is to bounce back."

Fortunately, we were alone in a room reserved for working, gossiping, and complaining about anything to do with education. No one, besides Nabila, must know I was failing.

Nabila, a petite, energetic woman, listened as I gave highlights of the class from hell: swearing, off-topic conversations, and disrespect. I was partly to blame; I didn't know how to get teens to work, nor how to discipline them.

"Jen, you taught at a Catholic school before this, right?" she asked.

I nodded.

"Students can't be lazy there. It's not like that here. But that doesn't mean these kids are bad. You just have to figure out how to work with them."

I thought back on my days at Saint Dominique, a Catholic elementary school in Casablanca, Morocco where I'd studied for three years, and where no one misbehaved. Initially I hated school, not knowing a word of French, but after three months of immersion, I became fluent. Nabila related to my experiences; as a child, she had attended a Catholic school in Beirut.

"My students are rude to me," I said. "Michael even cursed."

"Swearing isn't as bad as it once was," said Nabila. "Norms have changed. They're challenging you because you're a new teacher. They realize you don't know what you're doing and take advantage of that. Don't get discouraged. You'll learn how to control them. I'll help."

Then, she peppered me with questions about the previous day's lesson: Had I printed out the slides for them to take notes and required them to read sentences on the PowerPoint? Had I given them an informal assessment at the end of class?

I admitted I hadn't done that—nor did I know what an informal assessment was.

"It's a mini-quiz," she said. "It's a way to check students have learned the material. It's not worth many points, but it will hurt their grade if they don't do it. You should include at least one informal assessment in each lesson."

"I have to give them a quiz every day?" I said, shocked.

"It's not like when we grew up in the 70s and 80s," said Nabila. "We just worked because that's what you did. It's different now. Students love getting points—and current pedagogical theory supports this type of assessment."

I nibbled at my turkey and cheese sandwich, glumly thinking how I would be spending hours grading mediocre work from students I didn't like.

"So, what's an informal assessment for a PowerPoint?" I asked.

"Writing sentences using the vocabulary they just learned," she said. "Remember, you're not at a private school with only smart and motivated kids. Some students here won't go to college, others will have difficulty passing French. Our job isn't to train them to become scholars, though I'm sure a few of them will."

I sighed. It was time I took Nabila's advice to heart. "I'll include one," I said.

"Do it tomorrow," she said. "This can't wait. Leslie is observing you next week."

Since I was a non-tenured teacher, the world language supervisor would observe me three times that year to determine if I had the skills necessary to educate high schoolers. I was already dreading the first observation on October second. "Leslie will see me as a bad teacher," I said.

"No, she won't," said Nabila. "You just have to keep the kids busy. Don't spend too long on any one activity. Teenagers get bored easily. Let me see your lesson plans."

"I can't control my students," I said, handing her my lessons. "They're like feral cats."

Nabila laughed. "You're funny, Jen. But seriously, you must make them believe French is fun. Make the lesson relevant to their lives. They're very self-centered at this age. They're wondering why they should care about French."

*Teaching here was much more complicated than at the Catholic school. Could I change enough in a few days to impress Leslie?*

Nabila silently read my lesson plans. I watched as she rewrote most of my lesson. With a red pen, she slashed sentences, dashing off ideas in the margins.

"I'm not doing anything right," I said discouragingly, glancing at the paper splattered with blood red ink.

Within fifteen minutes, she created a lesson with a dialogue and exercises from a *C'est à Toi 2* textbook. "Last year, Leslie made us get rid of textbooks," she admitted. "But I managed to keep a few copies. Don't ever tell her."

*What was wrong with using a textbook written by experts? Certainly, I should include my own materials, but a complete ban on textbooks seemed ridiculous.*

I read Nabila's notes: "Write on the board the lesson's objective: to learn vocabulary associated with farm animals, comparing cultural differences between farms in America and France."

"Can't I just say we're learning about animals?" I asked Nabila. "Do I really need to write that all down?"

Nabila, who had a degree in education, was familiar with

what I called "pedagogical mumbo jumbo." "Jen, it's what the state wants. Let's just follow their guidelines. Schools are under attack for not teaching kids enough, and this is one example of a regulation that shows we know what we're doing. Evidently, we need to improve our schools, though I think we're doing just fine."

"By the way, my students want me to reteach French 1," I said. "They said they didn't learn anything last year. Should I do that?"

"No, but go slow with them," she advised. "Cathy wasn't as conscientious as you are—and Leslie hated her."

Nabila glanced at the clock; the bell would ring soon. "Can't you come to my class when Leslie's there?" I pleaded jokingly. "Or better yet, you teach my class that day."

Nabila laughed. "Relax. You have a great lesson. You'll do fine."

I wasn't so sure. The students had already taken charge, but, for Nabila, I would try.

# Millennials

As a baby boomer, I was puzzled about teaching late millennials, those born in the mid-1990s. They had grown up with the Internet, playing video games, surfing online, and using cell phones. As kids, they discovered Google, Facebook, YouTube, and Nintendo—and at school they learned how to navigate computers. Their brains were wired differently than mine. I was in my 30s when I started using computer technology.

In the classroom, I needed to adapt to teaching this generation. I discovered they challenged the hierarchical status quo, showed an intuitive knowledge of technology, placed importance on tasks rather than time, appreciated relationships with superiors, and valued meaningful motivation.

## Teaching Millennials

**Embrace technology, but don't let it dominate lessons.**

It's fine to ask students to take notes on paper and open a textbook.

Include online educational games they love.

Don't emphasize memorizing facts when the answer is clicks away.

Instead focus on interpretation and problem solving.

**Use real-world examples.**

Kids understand concepts better if they have practical applications.

**Give a lesson's main points in two to three minutes.**

Kids have limited attention spans. Don't lecture.

**Strike a balance in each lesson.**

Aim to inform, entertain, and interact with students.

# Chapter Two

# UNDER ATTACK

I stood at the classroom door, anxiously waiting for my students. My stomach churned and mind raced about how to survive an observation from Leslie. I repeated to myself: "I must do well; Nabila believes in me. I can handle these kids—It's only 50 minutes. Then they can go back to their chaotic teenage selves."

As usual, Michael was the first to enter.

"Bonjour, Michel. *Enleve tes écouteurs*," I said, gesturing for him to remove his earbuds.

He hastily passed by me. "I ain't understanding anything you say," he said snarkily.

*Thank God Leslie hadn't yet arrived. He'd defied authority by not doing what I asked. Administrators would frown on this.*

More students sauntered into the room, chattering and chewing gum. I greeted them, suppressing a feeling of dread that my fate would be sealed that day. Leslie entered the classroom, a notebook and pen in hand. The bell clanged. Quick! I needed the students to settle down.

"*Bon, on commence*," I announced, moving toward the blackboard. "*Ici, il y a la leçon qu'on fait aujourd'hui.*"

I pointed to the board where I had written that day's objectives—learning farm animal vocabulary words. Students continued to chat. Leslie plopped down in a student desk in the back, depositing a notebook in front of her.

"Meghan, *arrête de parler avec* Amanda," I said, signaling her to close her mouth.

"Why are you picking on me? Everyone else is talking too," she said.

Students talking back to me was nothing new, but I didn't want it to happen in front of Leslie. It showed disrespect. The dirty dozen were behaving normally, oblivious to an administrator with power to punish them—or fire me.

"*J'ai un dialogue pour vous*," I said, handing out a packet.

Only Elizabeth and Aravind thumbed through the packet; the others continued their social hour. I considered leaving the classroom and telling them that when I returned, I expected them to work. But I'd tried that before, and it hadn't worked.

"*Regardez les personnes dans le dialogue*," I said, showing them an image of people at a farm. "*Ils vont à la ferme.*"

Meghan looked with disdain at the paper with a picture of teenagers visiting a farm during the summer. "This girl has the ugliest clothes and hairstyle."

Amanda yelled out that she agreed. I didn't squelch the outbursts. Instead, I called for volunteers to read the dialogue.

"How old is this dialogue anyway?" said Meghan. "No one looks like that now."

In the back of the room, Leslie scribbled. Five minutes of class had passed. No one was working—except me.

Suddenly, Stephanie walked in. "I had to see my history teacher about something; that's why I'm late," she announced.

I let her sit down without repercussions. Leslie shook her head. I instantly knew I'd made a huge mistake.

"Who'd like to play the roles of Marian and Jean-Claude?" I asked, praying two students would volunteer.

Stephanie, who already spoke French, cried out that she

would, and urged the boys—either Michael or Aravind—to join her. Aravind agreed to play the role of the brother. Finally, students were engaged.

Stephanie's pronunciation was excellent, but Aravind struggled, so I occasionally corrected his mispronunciations. He didn't get discouraged or lash out at me for correcting him, and for that I was grateful. Michael undoubtedly would have felt offended by my repeated requests for correct pronunciation. He didn't like to be told what to do.

Much to my surprise, students listened to their peers. For the first time that period, I relaxed, realizing I'd done something right.

But that didn't last long. Students couldn't answer the comprehension questions—even after I defined new vocabulary words and we reread the dialogue. Leslie was smiling mischievously like the Cheshire Cat; I couldn't tell if she approved or disapproved of what I was doing.

"With a partner, try to answer the questions," I said. "Reread the dialogue. Translate it. We'll correct the exercise in five minutes."

As they worked, I circulated around the room. Sadly, few groups were working, and I scolded them—in English. Leslie frowned as she dashed off notes on her notepad.

Only one group made any effort; I praised those two students.

"I need to use the bathroom," said Aravind. "Can I go now?

"You should finish your work first."

"But it's an emergency," he insisted.

"After you get the work done, you can go."

Finally, Aravind started working.

Leslie leaned back in her seat; her voluminous belly protruding. Why was she now so relaxed? Was I wrong in telling a student he must finish work before using the restroom?

I asked Stephanie and Meghan to read their answers out loud; they did so without arguing. I beamed with joy; they had saved the lesson for me. But Leslie, in the back, grimaced.

I announced that we'd do a listening exercise.

"What's that?" cried out Michael, getting up from his desk to stretch.

"We've never done that before," exclaimed Stephanie.

"What are we supposed to do?" said Aravind timidly, having forgotten his supposedly urgent need to urinate.

After the cacophony of voices, I explained how they'd hear a statement and if it was logical, they would write *Oui* and if it was illogical, they'd write *Non*. For example, if I said "*On joue aux échecs dans la neige*," that would be *Non* because one doesn't play chess in the snow.

A barrage of cross talk bombarded me. "You can play chess anywhere!" "What's chess?" "Does anyone here play chess?" A loud boom of "No" echoed from the class.

*Boy, how different I am from them. I'd played chess in third grade. Couldn't they be polite and ask me to explain what it was?*

I didn't give up, continuing with the listening exercise. They complained that I spoke too fast, they didn't know the words, and the exercise was too difficult. Their neediness overwhelmed me; I no longer eyed Leslie. I had to calm them down, and that meant helping them define vocabulary words.

As a "closure activity," I asked students to write down three sentences using the new vocabulary words. Which animals did they like? Which ones did they want to see? Which ones lived in the forest, sea, or mountains? I glanced at the clock—only seven minutes until the end of the day.

"If you don't finish it in class, you will have to do it for homework," I threatened.

With that declaration, students started to pack up their backpacks, chat with their friends, and ask to use the bathroom. They said they'd do the work at home, but I knew half of them would blow it off.

Leslie looked shocked; evidently, I'd committed another mistake. At last the bell rang, but not before several students had started lining up in front of the door, anxious to leave, saying that they needed every second to make it to the bus on time. Would Leslie scold me for not keeping them busy all fifty minutes?

Leslie struggled to push her large frame out of the desk onto her feet. "I'll send you a write-up of your evaluation next week," said Leslie, leaving the room. "We'll schedule a time to talk about it."

I almost told her not to rush the write-up. Better yet, could I retake the observation? My students were always requesting a retake of a quiz or test. Couldn't I also get another evaluation?

"Sure, we'll talk later," I said, shutting the door behind her, suppressing tears about a failed lesson, fearful of a failed career.

The following week, Leslie emailed me a scathing evaluation. I read it in the faculty room during my free period. She blasted me for allowing students to blurt out answers without raising their hand, chatting to each other, and entering the class late without penalty. She noted that it was against the law to deny students bathroom privileges during class. Students were not engaged in the lesson and there wasn't a positive rapport between the students and me. I'd failed to earn the respect and trust of my students. She recommended I meet with Nabila to learn how to teach. Didn't she know I was already doing that?

Tears welled in my eyes. I needed to leave the school. I couldn't teach my French 2 period 7 class that day. I resented them. But because I couldn't leave early, I took refuge in a faculty bathroom and splashed away signs of distress.

At lunch, I showed Nabila the report. "I've never gotten such a bad evaluation," I said, my voice quivering. "I always try to do well at work. I don't want to get fired."

I sounded pathetic and vulnerable. Why had I ever left journalism? Even with lower pay, the Catholic school didn't look so bad after working at Northern.

Nabila lifted my spirits, saying all my shortcomings could be rectified with a little guidance, time, and patience. After all, I worked hard, cared about doing a good job, and was fluent in French. Besides, she asked, what would I do all day without work? She couldn't picture me cooking and cleaning; I didn't divulge my passion for writing.

"You'll get through this," she said, patting my back, as she nibbled on crackers with hummus. "You have what it takes to be a great teacher. What were Leslie's recommendations for improvements?"

"Everything."

She shook her head. "No, Jen, you did a lot well. But what you must do is build relationships with these students. You must start to like them. They are testing you—as they do all new teachers—but you can turn them around to make them like you."

"How do I do that?" I asked, sipping my Diet Coke.

"You've got to have fun in the classroom," she said. "Make it seem like the classroom is your favorite place. Laugh occasionally. Have a sense of humor with the kids. I know you can be funny. Don't be afraid to show more of yourself."

This was counter to what I'd learned during teacher training.

I was taught to be stern, strict, and unapproachable the first three months—and never smile. In that way, the logic went, students would be too scared to misbehave.

"I can try, but it might create even more chaos," I said.

"No, the students will see that you're enjoying yourself, so they will too."

First, to build a positive rapport with teenagers, I had to get to know every student in class: what hobbies they had, what motivated them to work, and what scared them. Nabila recommended I take a class period to help them write short, simple sentences in French about themselves—and then have them read them out loud.

"You've got to start liking your classes," she said, sitting as straight as a board. "Until that happens, they won't respect you."

Then, she ordered me to develop a seating chart. I had to separate friends—and put silent types next to chatty ones—and move desks into a semi-circle so that everyone was facing each other. No one could hide in class.

I sighed. I didn't have much faith in turning around this class. They were set in their ways. They had decided I was powerless to change the classroom's dynamics.

"I'm not sure it's going to work," I said.

"Of course, it will," said Nabila, adding that every day I had to include an informal assessment that was graded.

"I've been trying to do that," I said.

"Every week, you must have a game," she ordered, peeling a banana. "Perhaps every Friday. Say it's 'Fun Friday'—particularly if they've worked hard all week."

I smiled. A game. That would be fun.

"That sounds good," I said.

"If students like you, they will work hard. They'll forgive you for minor lapses in organization, discipline, or forgetfulness."

So, was that the winning formula? "I'll try," I said meekly.

"Tell Leslie that you're adjusting to teaching at both the middle school and high school. I'll continue to mentor you. She'll see how serious you are about this job."

"I don't fit the model of a teacher."

"Jen, stop. You're good. Some of the kids are very bad—and now Leslie wants you to take charge. That's it."

"I have until February to improve," I said. "That's my next observation."

She offered me half of her chocolate chip muffin, saying she needed to lose weight. I savored the pastry's sweetness and softness, gradually feeling that maybe, just maybe, someday I would see how satisfying teaching could be.

## Evaluating Teachers

It's part of most people's job: the yearly evaluation that can determine time spent at a workplace. At schools, it serves a purpose to highlight—and sometimes reward—teachers who show the spark, commitment, and energy to educate. It also targets educators who fail to teach students.

Districts use different performance evaluation models to determine a teacher's effectiveness. Traditionally, a supervisor or principal observes how a teacher handles a class, and considers lesson plans, student achievement, student surveys, and professionalism in an evaluation.

Many use these evaluation frameworks: The Danielson Group, Stronge and Associates, LSI Marzano Center, McREL International, and the University of Washington.

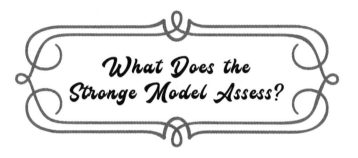

## What Does the Stronge Model Assess?

**PROFESSIONAL KNOWLEDGE**

Know the subject matter and curriculum.

**INSTRUCTIONAL PLANNING**

Develop lessons that consider standards and curriculum, and strategies to engage students.

**INSTRUCTIONAL DELIVERY**

Be enthusiastic and energetic in class.

**ASSESSMENT OF LEARNING**

Give students quizzes and tests, and informal assessments to gauge student progress.

### LEARNING ENVIRONMENT

Provide a respectful, positive, safe environment.

### PROFESSIONALISM

Dress and act appropriately, fulfill professional development hours, work well with colleagues.

### STUDENT PROGRESS

Show that students learn material by assessing at the beginning and end of the school year.

# Chapter Three

# JEOPARDY

What should I do to get to know my students better? I rejected asking them to write a paragraph about themselves in French; they'd just resort to Google Translate to complete the assignment. I thought about assigning a short speaking assignment about their hobbies, families, and classes, but with their weak foundation, they'd be lost. Instead, I would focus on creating fun activities, and as they played, I'd learn a thing or two about them. During my alternate route class—a state-sponsored program for adults to get certified to teach—I remembered how one student had made a Jeopardy game out of cloth. It was great. Lively. Fun. Engaging. This tool would turn around my class.

That weekend I bought some green felt, a wooden dowel rod, and some ribbon, took out my Singer sewing machine, and started making the board. I sewed on colorful pockets, slid the rod in an opening on top, and wrote questions about daily routine on index cards that I stuffed in the pockets. Hours later, my board was complete. Voila! A masterpiece. My three children thought it was cool. The students would love it. They would think it was a great way to review for a quiz. And, unlike the PowerPoint, I could reuse it to prepare for other assessments. No longer would I be regarded as a failure; Nabila would be pleased with me.

"Finally, something interesting," murmured Megan, eyeing the board.

"Did you make that?" asked Stephanie perceptively.

I nodded.

"Are we going to play a game today?" Michael blurted out.

I smiled as if they were my favorite teenagers, then briefly explained the game's rules.

"Everyone knows Jeopardy, right?" I asked.

They nodded. "One person says the answer, and if they get it wrong, they don't get points," said Stephanie.

"Yes, and then the question goes to the next team," I said. "We're playing it a little differently from the game on TV."

"You're talking way too much," Amanda said. "We know how to play Jeopardy."

*Wow, that was rude, but was it worth reprimanding her? I wanted this to be the lesson that students remembered with joy.*

"When are we going to start?" Sara yelled out.

"We get this," asserted Aravind, fidgeting in his seat.

With that, the game began—and chaos soon followed. Students in each group yelled out answers, loudly debating which answer was correct. They blasted me with questions about whether they could use their textbooks and notes to find the answers. One group accused the other group of cheating by using their cell phones. They bickered over who won the point.

I stood paralyzed, cringing at the mayhem in the room—though at least the students were engaged. I called for quiet to clarify rules. They only half-listened, the procedures coming too late to change the circus-like atmosphere. I was losing my good humor and wanted to quit the game, but I knew students would revolt if I cut this fun lesson short. How wild students could get under improper leadership. I was crushed and I couldn't help but reflect on my successful days at the Catholic school.

Couldn't Northern students resolve problems as calmly and

politely as Sacred Heart students? Was it worth doubling my salary to work at a job I hated? Sister Lillian's parting words haunted me. "Public schools don't have the same caliber of student as we do. You might have problems with attitude, and the kids won't respect you. It's tough out there."

She was right. I was not prepared to handle these teenagers— even with Nabila's help. What had the education guru Harry Wong said about controlling attitude-prone teens from different socio-economic backgrounds? At a summer workshop, Wong emphasized clear procedures and rules from the first day as outlined in his book, *The First Days of School: How to Be an Effective Teacher.* Obviously, I'd failed to do that. I regretted not taking copious notes during my teaching training program to be certified for public school. Then public school teachers had lamented how their classrooms were filled with undisciplined, unruly teenagers— and our teacher provided strategies to deal with them. I'd not taken their advice to heart since at the time, I'd been teaching at a Catholic school with disciplined, hardworking girls; I never imagined life could be so different in public schools.

The jeopardy game dissolved into anarchy: A few students dropped out, complaining questions were too hard; another couple dominated the game by gaining point after point; and several looked on with interest, seemingly relishing the disorder. The bell rang. I folded the felt Jeopardy game and shoved it in its bag, vowing to never play it again with my French 2 students. I hadn't gotten to know any one of my students better—and I didn't feel warm and fuzzy around them. No, we still didn't like each other. Nabila would be disappointed. I didn't want to tell her I again had failed. At what point might she give up on me?

★ ★ ★

I met Nabila in the cafeteria during her lunchroom duty. I had vowed not to cry or complain about my students. Instead, I calmly explained that the Jeopardy game had been a disaster and asked for advice.

Nabila rummaged through her flowered lunch bag to retrieve a salad with nuts, dried cranberries, and tomato. "Jen, you can make the game fun. You just need to implement and enforce clear rules and procedures. You're too lenient with them. You have to be firm."

I jotted down notes in my planner. I felt like a student on the verge of getting an F, who'd need tons of tutoring to pass the class.

She recommended I appoint one spokesperson per group to give the final answer and set a twenty-second time limit to answer a question. The game must be fast-paced to avoid long discussions. Also, stop the game immediately if students become too wild—and give them a worksheet to complete instead.

"They much prefer a game to a worksheet, so they should stop misbehaving."

I sighed. "I wish I'd known that earlier."

"They were interested in the lesson, right? Leslie always talks about engaging students, and you did that with the Jeopardy game. That's a big step forward! So, now you just must work on classroom management and you're golden."

Trust Nabila to find the positive in the previous day's lesson. "These students are way too unruly for me."

Nabila nibbled on her salad. "You just got a bad bunch this year—and on top of it, you're new. They take advantage of you. Every day, show them you're in charge."

I felt like running off to a cave and hibernating until the final bell in June; I didn't know if I could ever turn the class around—

and it wasn't even Halloween. "Kids are so different now from when I was growing up."

Then, Nabila and I shared our experiences of attending Catholic schools in Beirut and Casablanca, where we'd avoided being spanked or having our fingers hit with a ruler. When we were students, we didn't dare misbehave, afraid of being punished for any minor infraction. Our mantra had been: Do the work, don't complain, and don't act up. We dreaded the thought of a principal telling our parents about our misdeeds, which would mean more punishment. It was just wiser to do what we were told—and that meant respecting teachers. Neither Nabila nor I had known anything about pedagogical methodology or learning styles—not like today's students, who claimed to be analytical or kinesiological learners. As students, we'd never thought our opinion mattered to teachers with years of experience in life and learning. But that was decades earlier. Now, Nabila and I were teaching in a new era with new norms.

"When I was a teenager, I wanted to learn," I said. "I liked school."

"Some kids here really like learning," said Nabila. "Lots of my students plan on going to college and they want to do well. They're kind to me."

The lunchroom smelled of greasy French fries and fatty hamburgers. Students sat on metal benches in the brightly lit room. All was in order. No one was lashing out at an adult. How could I avoid confrontation in my classroom? How could I get my students to be kind to me?

"Why don't you observe one of my classes?" said Nabila. "You'll pick up on how to act around students."

Yes, the five years I'd taught in a Catholic school, and years before then with the Peace Corps in Niger, hadn't prepared me for Northern. Nabila would be my buoy as I struggled to stay afloat.

### How to Manage Students

**Get to know students.**

Establish a rapport with them. The more they respect you, the harder they'll work.

**Keep students working.**

Students are more likely to misbehave when they have nothing to do.

**Establish clear rules.**

Enforce rules fairly and consistently.

**Hold students accountable.**

Give them a grade every class. Don't say which activity you're grading.

**Listen to students' concerns.**

Understand they have their point of view—even if it's not yours.

**Open up about yourself.**

Students behave better if they know and like their teacher.

**Be flexible.**

Accept that students—and teachers—have off days; adjust lessons accordingly.

**Talk to other teachers.**

Ask colleagues for help when working with a problem student.

**Create engaging lessons.**

Teach lessons you are enthusiastic about—your energy will motivate them to learn.

**Partner with parents and guardians.**

They can be your biggest ally—or adversary—so communicate regularly with them.

## Chapter Four

# A MURKY FUTURE

That summer, exhausted after teaching a year at Northern, I put on hold looking for another job. Instead, I spent whole days caring for my three children, hanging out at the community pool, town library, and beach, and then travelling with them to France. Soon, I would have to start applying for jobs, but this break was essential for regaining a sense of well-being.

Throughout the summer, I reflected on my life's imbalance: I had too little quality time with my children. Romantic pursuits had been sidelined. Somehow, I had to reinvent myself professionally, while keeping parenting a priority. I couldn't keep my mind from wandering back to my first true love—journalism. As a Peace Corps volunteer in Niger, I'd discovered how much I enjoyed writing, penning stories about my experiences living and teaching in one of the world's poorest countries. After my return to America, I earned a graduate degree in journalism from Columbia University, which launched me into a decade-long career writing for newspapers and magazines. Deep down, I was hoping I could return to the profession, but I couldn't ignore why I had left it in the first place.

★ ★ ★

Four years earlier, as a reporter for a business magazine, I thought I knew exactly what I wanted from my life, until the morning I started bawling in the newsroom.

Tears gushed down my face, blurring my vision as I struggled to read my interview notes for an article about a local accounting firm. The clock was ticking. In an hour, my editor would scold me for tying up the editorial process and accuse me of slacking off.

*Come on, just start typing.*

Certainly, I could do that. After all, I had penned stories for the business journal for almost two years—and I never missed a deadline. The adrenaline always kicked in when I had to produce copy.

I closed my eyes, searching for a Zen-like state that would allow sentences and paragraphs to flow effortlessly. At one time, the newsroom had been my salvation, a place where I'd bonded with the all-male editorial staff while my marriage dissolved. My husband and I had separated after we couldn't agree on matters, including our children's bedtime. But now, new owners were bombarding reporters with requirements for more stories. I couldn't hack the added workload. I felt like a failure.

Hunkered down at my desk, I squelched my sobs so as not to be overheard whimpering like a trapped animal. Mark, in the cubicle to my right, was conducting a phone interview. No sound

came from Scott on my left. He was probably out on assignment.
I was safe from prying eyes and ears. Marshall was too far away to
hear me, sequestered in his own private office. I could escape
without anyone noticing. The article about Melissa Rosenberg's
successful accounting firm would just have to wait.

The fresh air would clear my mind—and blanch my rose-
colored cheeks and bloodshot eyes. Gingerly, I peered over my
cubicle as I wiped my tears and stood.

"Where are you going?" Scott poked his head above the cubicle wall.

"On a walk." *What the hell! Why wasn't he out?* I lowered my
head so he couldn't see my face.

"Is everything okay?" he said.

The usual "fine" that spilled from my lips regardless of my
troubles at home refused to come. "Not really. I should go."

Scott approached me, a look of concern on his face. "Maybe
you want to talk about it. I can join you on a walk."

"Don't you have a story to write?" I asked. I wasn't sure I
should confide in him. For a long time—ever since my husband
and I had separated—I'd taken care of problems on my own.

"That can wait. I've never seen you this upset."

"I need to get out of this place," I said, sniffling. "I can't go
for long though. John wants the story on Rosenberg."

Scott grabbed his windbreaker from the coat rack; we descended the narrow staircase in the three-story, downtown building.

Outside, the warm spring air refreshed me. I glanced at the
cloudless blue sky. It wouldn't be long before we were blasted
with heat and humidity, just around the time my divorce would
be finalized in late June.

"At least it's not raining," I said, in a feeble attempt to start a
conversation.

"I can see why you're anxious with all the changes at the magazine," said Scott, a thirty-something wannabe hipster. "I'm feeling it too."

Trust Scott to cut to the chase. "It's insane what they want us to do now. I can't write three stories a week and two or three briefs every morning."

Scott nodded. "You can do it. Just interview fewer sources—and pick stories that are easy hits."

"I'm already doing that," I said. "And I'm completely stressed. I don't want to cover events superficially, but that's exactly what we're now doing."

"We had it good with George."

George, a former *Time* writer and founder of the business journal, had trusted his staff to cover industries in depth. He gave us time to craft insightful, analytical stories. The new owners believed readers wanted shorter stories—and more of them.

"Why couldn't George have waited another couple of years to sell the paper?" I lamented.

George's wife had complained about being the paper's office manager and had convinced her husband it was time to retire to their Block Island home. It had taken George two years to find a buyer who agreed to his terms and all but one condition: maintaining a reasonable workload for reporters.

"The new owners don't seem that bad," said Scott, his curly blond hair framing his face. "You'll get used to them. You're a hard worker."

"I can't work until eight at night. I need to pick up my kids at six."

"Could you come in early in the morning?"

"Not really. I get them ready to leave for school at 8:15."

"That's tough."

As we walked rapidly, I looked at the beautiful tree-lined street. Ash trees stretched upward, their branches strong and sturdy as if they could handle any disturbance.

"I just don't know if it's worth it," I said. "Maybe I should start looking for another job."

Scott sighed. "I'd hate to see you go. You're a good reporter. And you like journalism."

The sniffling resumed. "You're right about that."

Scott recommended that I not rush a decision. With time, he felt I could adjust to the workload, though initially I'd need to work longer days. Was there a babysitter who could help out for a month or two?

His suggestions made sense to me. But would I ever get used to cranking out three stories a week while raising three young children?

Scott opened the building door, gesturing for me to enter. "If something's bothering you, I'm always up for another walk."

*What a sweetie!* I nodded, almost bursting into tears again. We climbed the staircase to the second floor. "Is my face red?" I asked. It always turned red when I cried.

"A little. But it's fine." He patted me gently on the back before returning to his cubicle.

In the upstairs' bathroom, I splashed water on my face and caked powder on my checks to hide signs of distress. Scott would keep quiet about my issues. No one else needed to know I was drowning at my job.

Journalists'
Salaries

(Median wages in 2020)

**Editors: $50,000**

**Reporters: $36,000**

*Source: Bureau of Labor Statistics*

*Chapter Five*

# SHOULD I TEACH?

In the following weeks I churned out a slew of stories, viewing myself as an assembly line robot without respite from production.

I no longer took hour-long lunches with colleagues or analyzed company reports. I interviewed sources in less than thirty minutes—on the phone, never in person—and cranked out each story in an hour. Bathroom breaks were limited to five minutes, twice a day. I degenerated into an overworked machine, my worth measured in efficiency and productivity, not quality.

But I managed to leave the office at precisely 5:00 p.m. I couldn't keep my kids waiting at their after-school care program. The few times I'd been late, I'd gotten dirty looks from the staff, and a warning that if my lateness continued, I'd be charged extra. My children deserved a mom taking care of them for at least a few waking hours. Their father, very occupied with his career in business, could never pick them up by 6:00 p.m.

At home, I quickly prepared simple dinners: macaroni and cheese, ready-made meatballs with pasta, and Hamburger Helper. As the kids got ready for bed, I snapped at them when they dawdled. Couldn't they hurry up? I needed a few minutes to read newspapers to get ideas for future business stories. I'd lose my patience when Patrick, eight, couldn't find his pajamas, or Emily, ten, refused to go to bed, or Nicholas, nine, teased his brother. Why couldn't they just behave like little angels? I was too exhausted to handle even the slightest misbehavior.

Regularly, I fantasized about quitting my job. Why not move to my mother's mountain retreat in Lake Tahoe where the children and I could live rent-free? There, I could write for the weekly newspaper, *The Bonanza*. But my children's father wanted to see his kids regularly and would be devastated if we moved away. Besides, the divorce agreement prevented me from relocating unless I found a job with a comparable salary. A weekly newspaper wouldn't cut it—nor could I justifiably uproot my kids from all they'd known and loved.

So, I had two choices: adjust to the demands at *The Business Chronicle* or find a different local job. Short term, I busted my butt to hand in stories on time and hoped the stress wouldn't lead to a nervous breakdown. Long term, I worried I would become a basket case. But I wasn't thinking that far into the future. Take it day-by-day. Keep in check my exhaustion by not overscheduling myself on weekends. Most importantly, maintain a positive attitude that I could do it all.

One day at work, after a restless night of pondering my future, I approached Bill, a senior writer and editor. The door was open to his private office, meaning he'd welcome visitors.

"How can I help you?" asked Bill, a scholarly gentleman with a law degree, looking up from his computer. "Sit down. Are you okay? I hardly see you these days."

"I don't know how much longer I can take this job," I said, dabbing at my eye. "I'm overworked and stressed out here. I lash out at my kids. I'm always rushing."

"Here's a tissue," said Bill, reaching for a box of Kleenex.

"I barely have time to breathe," I said, wiping away a tear.

"It's the new regime," said Bill, leaning back in his chair. "They're cracking down on us. You're keeping up. John hasn't complained about you." Bill's kind blue eyes showed sympathy with my plight. "You're not thinking about quitting, are you?"

"No, I need a job," I said. "You remember that I'm getting a divorce next month."

"You could change your mind," he said, pushing back thin blond hair.

"I don't think I will. We haven't lived together for years."

"You never know."

"I feel so drained. I used to have fun in this place. Now it's a grind."

"I agree. Our new leader doesn't want analysis. It's tough for me too, but I'm getting used to it. Just report less and write more. That's the winning formula."

I smiled, appreciating the simplicity of his solution. "It sounds like you're talking about winning a car race."

He laughed. "Jen, it's hard for you because you're under time constraints. I don't have the responsibility of children. This might not be the right job for you. Maybe you should consider teaching."

"Teaching?" I asked incredulously. *Didn't he know how I'd disliked teaching in Niger as a Peace Corps volunteer after college graduation? That had been twenty years ago—perhaps I'd never told him about that experience.*

"What's wrong with teaching? Remember how your predecessor Sarah left to teach Spanish at a public school?"

I nodded. "She likes her new job?"

"From what I understand, she's very happy. She earns more

money, works fewer hours, comes home when her kids do, and gets better retirement and health care benefits. I don't think she misses this place one bit."

"Her kids are young, right?"

"I think so. She was always pressed for time—just like you. Now, she's found a way to balance raising a family while earning a living."

I rubbed my forehead, thinking about the benefits of teaching, but my heart rejected such a move. "I like reporting and writing."

"For the past month, you haven't been happy. You don't smile anymore and I can't remember the last time I heard you laugh."

He was right about that. I wasn't enjoying life. I felt like a slave to the newspaper. It wasn't fair to my children to devote so much energy to my profession and so little to them. The years would zip by; I didn't want to be an absent mom. How many sacrifices was this job worth? Weren't my kids as important as my job?

Yet a large part of my identity came from being a journalist, and for years I'd loved my job. I'd committed to the profession after getting a master's degree in journalism at Columbia.

"You know Bill, I used to wake up super excited to go to work. I loved this place. I looked forward to seeing you guys and reporting on companies. It was the best."

Bill frowned. "It is what it is. I'll stay around for a while. But I'm also thinking about exploring other opportunities."

So it wasn't just me who was considering a change. "Where would you go?"

"Perhaps Washington. I've been contacting government agencies. Maybe I could be a spokesperson or work in communications."

"That'd be quite a move."

"It's tough breaking into government work. But for you, teaching might not be that bad. You could teach English—or French. I seem to remember you speak French. There will be job openings this fall."

As Bill talked about the benefits of being an educator, I could see how it might work. I had a degree in English and I'd learned French as a child, though I hadn't spoken it in years.

"So your French is little rusty," said Bill. "You'll remember it. You're going to know so much more than anyone in high school."

I glanced at my watch—ten minutes had passed and what had I accomplished? No words had been written, no source interviewed, but Bill's insight gave me hope I could find a way out of my difficult situation. Perhaps I should consider teaching. It would provide me with a way to see my own kids more often. Surely, teaching wouldn't be nearly as stressful as the newsroom. Is it so important to be passionate about one's job when one has kids?

Nevertheless, I couldn't discount how my dad had encouraged me to find a profession I loved with interesting colleagues and tasks. After all, I'd be spending half of my waking hours there. I'd be miserable if I didn't like the work.

"Thanks, Bill, for your suggestions," I said, getting up. "I should get back to work."

"I'm glad you stopped by. By the way, I think you'd be a great teacher." His eyes twinkled.

"Really? Why?"

"You're personable—and fun—when you're not stressed out," he said.

## Discrepancies in Starting Teachers' Salaries

**$18,500:**

Lowest (several rural Pennsylvania districts)

**$41,163:**

Average in the U.S.

**$80,000:**

Highest (a California district)

*Source: NEA 2019-2020 Teacher Salary Benchmark report*

## Chapter Six

# GIRLS' WEEKEND

B ill's suggestion made me ponder the benefits of teaching, so one evening at home I searched the Internet to find out more about the profession. Salaries were decent in my state—a big plus—and a dozen public schools were looking for English or French teachers. But those required a teaching license—I didn't have one— and involved taking written and oral exams, enrolling in an Alternate Route teaching training program, and providing the state with documentation of college course work completed with a minimum GPA of 3.00. I could do all that, but it would take time. So much for making the big bucks at a public school job in September! Parochial and private schools didn't demand a teaching certificate, so I perused online employment sites for openings at schools within commuting distance, but none popped up. I felt relieved—I wasn't ready to end my days at the business journal—but also anxious, as I dwelled on the demands of balancing parenting with reporting.

By early August, just before a weekend visit from two childhood friends, I was convinced I'd be spending another year at *The Business Chronicle*. Schools started in less than a month, so districts had certainly finished hiring new staff. No need to anticipate a big change in my life. Instead, I'd enjoy reconnecting with Cathy and Vanessa after years of chatting only by phone, and without our kids it would be a true girls' getaway. We'd grown up in the suburbs outside Washington, DC, playing on the same street. Now serendipitously, as mothers, we reunited.

The next week Vanessa and Cathy arrived on my doorstep, excited to see my new home, visit the Statue of Liberty, and just hang out. As we sipped coffee in my kitchen, I moaned about being a middle-aged woman who should be sailing along professionally; instead, I was considering becoming a teacher. My kids were beginning to beg for more time with their father. Ouch, that hurt.

Cathy and Vanessa looked at me with sympathy, the room bathed in sunlight, promising a bright day ahead.

"It's not weird switching jobs in your 40s," said Vanessa, a 42-year-old from Baltimore. "I did it in nursing."

"It seems like you're ready for a change," said Cathy, her blue eyes gazing at me. "Journalism sounds super demanding for single moms. You'd be a great teacher."

*Bill from the office had said the same thing.*

"You're kind and caring—that's what kids need," piped in Vanessa, who had two daughters in middle school. "Besides, you'll have more time at home. How many vacation days do you have now? Fifteen?"

I nodded sadly. "Yes, that's not nearly enough."

★ ★ ★

They recommended I skip our planned day trip to the Statue of Liberty and instead apply to several schools for a teaching position, assuring me that school districts would post jobs in a mad rush to fill openings before Labor Day.

"You drove hours to see me," I said, nibbling an English muffin. "I want to hang out with you."

"Jen, we'll be okay," said Cathy, patting my back. "You don't need to see the Statue of Liberty again. Haven't you seen it ten times already? Jeez . . . just look for a job. Vanessa and I will be fine going without you."

Trust Cathy, a down-to-earth Bostonian and daughter of an Army general, to order me around. As an engineer, she had a precise, logical way of viewing the world. Vanessa, who sat next to her, nodded in agreement.

"That's not going to be fun," I said.

Cathy laughed. "It's got to be done. You've got to fix your own problems and not get distracted. I wish I had a job that allowed me to spend more time with Rachel and Alex. But I manage a staff, so that's not happening."

"So, why don't you go into teaching?" I asked.

Cathy reflected a moment, as if weighing the pros and cons of managing a division at an engineering company, as well as her teaching capabilities. "No, it's not for me. I don't think I'd enjoy working with teenagers. Besides, I'm settled where I am."

Vanessa, sipping her coffee, complained about her long

hours at the call center. "I get tired of giving medical advice to people I never see. Some of them are super obnoxious and rude. Maybe I should find a job where I actually meet patients—and don't work late."

"You could be a school nurse!" I said.

"The pay sucks!" said Vanessa. "I can't afford a pay cut—not now with another divorce."

Nine months after marrying Bob, Vanessa discovered he was an alcoholic; she couldn't live with someone who often came home drunk. Despite her pleas, Bob had refused to go to Alcoholics Anonymous. They were selling their boat—their last common asset—and once that was finalized, they'd file for divorce.

"I can't imagine how tough it's been for you," I said. "I can't understand why he didn't get help."

Vanessa looked wistful, as if reliving their once happy times together. "For a long time, he kept it hidden. It's a disease, and until he admits he has a problem, I can't do anything to make it better."

How well I remembered their wedding at their refurbished Northern Virginia home. They had spent months renovating the kitchen and fixing up the yard in preparation for taking their vows there.

"How sad," I said. "At your wedding, you two seemed like a perfect match."

Vanessa sighed. "Jen, life changes. You have to deal with it. I'm getting over it."

What great strength and resilience Vanessa showed in dealing with life's twists and turns. I could learn from her: Take action. Don't overanalyze situations. Move on.

"Vanessa and I should leave soon," piped in Cathy, glancing at her watch. "We don't want to get to Lady Liberty too late."

★ ★ ★

That evening, Vanessa and Cathy burst in through the kitchen door, exuberant after a day viewing exhibits about immigrants trekking to America. The smell of spaghetti sauce welcomed them. I mentioned I'd applied to two teaching jobs—one for French, the other English—at parochial schools.

"You only need one job," said Cathy. "Those Catholic schools are going to think you're the answers to their prayers."

I wasn't sure that was the case—I hadn't taught for twenty years, and I was a divorcée, a no-no for Catholics. "How was Ellis Island?" I asked, disappointed I hadn't spent the day with them.

"We mostly just hung out at the café," said Vanessa, with a grin on her face.

"We needed to catch up," said Cathy. "Let's open a bottle of wine. We'll toast to Jennifer soon getting a job in teaching!"

Around the kitchen table we reestablished our friendship, once long dormant, as we drank glass after glass of Yellow Tail chardonnay. Cathy and I expressed our support for Vanessa as she faced the prospect of another divorce, selling a $40,000 motorboat, and finding another mate. We chatted about the challenges and joys of raising children while working full time. Vanessa and Cathy assured me I'd get at least one job interview.

"Look, Jen," said Cathy. "It's August fifth. They need a French and English teacher in three weeks. They aren't going to quibble about your French not being perfect. You're super qualified."

"You're probably right," I said. "I have no idea what they pay."

"You're still getting alimony and child support, right?" asked Vanessa. "So you don't need to make the big bucks yet."

★ ★ ★

The next afternoon after a leisurely brunch, we hugged each other goodbye, promising to see each other again soon. The weekend had rejuvenated Vanessa, giving her the energy to handle an up-coming divorce, while Cathy mentioned how spending time away from her daughters made her appreciate them more. We were all going back to our routines—kids, work, home—but would mine stay the same? It was nerve-racking to think that if my friends were right, I could be starting a new profession in three weeks. I felt unsettled as I imagined myself in a new workplace, not knowing anyone, and unsure about how to teach. But no need to panic; I hadn't yet gotten an interview, and maybe I never would.

**American Schools**

**Public and Private (total)** — 130,930

**Elementary (K-6)** — 87,498

**Secondary (7-12)** — 26,727

**Combined (different levels)** — 15,804

**Other** — 901

*Source: National Center for Education Statistics (2017-18)*

## Who Are Our Teachers?

Women — 77%

Men — 23%

Average Age — 42

White — 80%

Average Years Teaching — 15

Master's Degrees — 51%

*Source: National Center for Education Statistics*

## Chapter Seven

# MY SANCTUARY

I couldn't wait to tell Cathy and Vanessa the good news: A Catholic school wanted to interview me for a high school French position.

"Can you believe it?" I exclaimed to Cathy over the phone. "I'm talking to the nuns next week."

"I knew you'd impress them," said Cathy.

I pictured Cathy standing in her Boston suburban colonial house, chopping vegetables as she prepared a salad with tomatoes and cucumbers from her garden. Her husband would be barbecuing chicken on the bluestone slate patio, where they'd eat dinner, a fire pit lit on this chilly evening.

"It was so quick," I said. "I applied only two days ago."

"They don't have time to mess around," said Cathy. "If you

don't accept the job, those kids won't have a French teacher. You're the answer to their prayers."

"But I don't remember any French!" I moaned.

"Jen, stop it. We already talked about this. Call your French speaking friend Geneviève. She'll help you out."

Trust Cathy to believe in me, even when I didn't.

I worried I didn't know enough about teenagers to work in a high school. But I would learn. I prided myself on being able to connect to all types of people. Relating to teenagers shouldn't be any different, right?

On my daily walk, the day before the interview, I called my friend Geneviève. Sometimes she didn't pick up the phone, overwhelmed with taking care of her two children, her husband, and her teaching job. She had a graduate degree in education and had taught for a decade at a bilingual public school. On the other hand, I never thought about language acquisition or pedagogy, nor had I taken any education classes.

"I need your help," I said as I neared the town's park. "I have an interview tomorrow for a job teaching French."

"French? Teaching?" said Geneviève. "You'll be fantastic!"

She reminded me how we were almost native speakers after learning the language as children in Morocco. She assured me French would come back to me quickly.

"Look, I'll interview you in French," said Geneviève.

With that, we entered the French-speaking world of my past, where I rattled off my qualifications for the job, teaching skills, and interest in the school. By the time I reached the park's bridge, my words were flowing effortlessly, the ache in my stomach gone.

"You sound great," said Geneviève. "No need to worry."

"What if they ask me something I don't know? Like how do you say, 'I scored a goal'?"

"It's *marquer un but*," she said. "But Jenny, they're not going to ask you that—and if they do, talk around it. This is a piece of cake."

"I might freeze up," I said.

"Jenny, you'll be fine. Relax. Take deep breaths."

"Maybe I should do yoga before the interview."

She laughed. "I have to pick up Mary Louise from the barn. Call me after the interview. You'll blow them away."

I pictured Geneviève driving her minivan to pick up her nine-year-old daughter who was horseback riding in the Virginia countryside. Despite a handful of challenging students, Geneviève liked teaching elementary school. She appreciated summers off and the ability to take her kids to practices, games, and sleepovers. Maybe I would be less frazzled with a similar schedule. Geneviève made me confident I'd ace the interview with Sister Lillian set for 11:00 a.m. the next day.

★ ★ ★

In the sanctity of her office, Sister Lillian sat behind a sturdy oak desk. She looked professional—like a businesswoman—in a boxy black blazer and skirt, but a little like a hippie in tan, worn Birkenstocks. A black cap and veil covered all but a few strands of gray hair. Piles of papers were stacked around her, a dated Dell computer to her left.

"So you're interested in teaching French," said Sister Lillian, her arms crossed in front of her.

"Yes, I am. I taught in the Peace Corps in West Africa, and in a school for adults in Switzerland," I said, anxiously breathing in the smell of coffee.

"That's fascinating," she said, looking at my resume. "I'm glad you believe in serving others."

I eyed the silver band around her ring finger: She was married to Christ.

"But you're now working at a magazine," she said, scrutinizing me through bifocals. "Why do you want to change professions?"

"I'm having a hard time balancing work and family. I have three children."

*No way was I going to mention my insecurities about teaching or my crying episodes in the newsroom.*

She wasn't bothered by the fact that I was divorced and Protestant. Evidently my predecessor, Renée, was Jewish. During World War II in France, the Catholic Church had sheltered Renée, and in gratitude for saving her life, she worked for the nuns.

"Classes are small here, and students are disciplined," she said. "That's not always the case at public schools."

"You must be proud of the school," I said.

Sister Lillian leaned back in her leather seat, smiling broadly. "We try to do what we can. We don't have enough money for everything we want—like new computers for staff."

*So I'd use a textbook and workbook more than online resources— at least initially.*

"By the way, I learned French at a Catholic school in Casablanca," I said. "That's where I learned how to study and work hard."

Sister Lillian nodded. "We want all our girls to get accepted into good colleges. Now you should talk to Karin. She teaches French part-time at the middle school."

Upstairs, as we walked through gray, artless corridors, I peered into classrooms with lifeless metal desks. The click from my heels echoed through the hallways, and I wished I had worn sandals like Sister Lillian's. I felt like an infidel in this calm, religious retreat, so unlike the newsroom's rippling tension. Could this sixty-five-year-old parochial school run by sisters become my new home?

Karin looked like a classy Parisian woman in a blue shift dress and flowered scarf around her neck. We conversed in French about children, home life, and experiences in France, and I sensed I was with a friend. She told me about the job: I would teach four or five levels of French and attend faculty meetings, religious services, and parent-teacher conferences. She had considered taking the job, but her kids were too young for her to be gone all day.

"You know, salaries aren't high," said Karin. "At public schools, you can easily make two to three times as much."

*Wow, that would be far more than what I earn as a journalist. Once child support and alimony ended, I should consider working at a public school, so I won't go broke.*

"For a few years, it'll be okay."

"Do you want the job?" she asked frankly. "I will recommend you. The sisters are easy to work with. You won't have problems with the girls—not like at public schools."

I hesitated. Should I confide in Karin that I was conflicted about leaving journalism—even temporarily? At one time I'd loved my profession, but I wasn't sure I did anymore since the place had become a grind. Certainly I would feel more relaxed and less pressured at this school. Besides, if I didn't like teaching, I could return to writing for a publication. Now I needed a job that balanced parenting with earning a living—and one that didn't result in tears and stress. I glanced at Karin, so peaceful and content while working and raising children, and I wanted to be like her. It would muddy the waters—and make a job offer unlikely—if I told her that accepting this job might change my life forever. Besides, couldn't I reinvent myself into an elegant, sophisticated French teacher whose students adored her?

"Tell the nuns that I would like to work here," I said.

★ ★ ★

At a going-away lunch at our favorite Thai restaurant, the guys at *The Business Chronicle* wished me well in my new endeavor. No one questioned why I was leaving a profession I loved; instead, they noted there were more jobs for educators than journalists and summers and holidays off couldn't be beat. As they handed me a plaque commemorating important events at the newspaper, I sensed I was making a mistake, embarking on an ill-prepared journey. Would I wake up excited to teach? Could I evolve into a respected, competent educator?

Teddy-bear-like Marshall hugged me as he wished me the best. I'd miss our lunchtime walks along the Raritan River! Bill, the pharmaceutical industry reporter, told me not to worry about my competency in French. I thanked Scott for listening to me as I decided what professional path to follow, and John, our illustrious editor, insisted I was making the right decision, given that I had three children.

My eyes teared up as I wished them all adieu. As we exited the restaurant, I realized that I might never see these wonderful men again. We were now on different journeys. I brushed away a few tears from my face, nervous about the path ahead. Teaching just had to work out—at least for a few years.

## Private Schools (K-12)

Enrollment: 5 million

**Types of Schools**

Catholic: 35%

Non-religious: 26%

Unaffiliated religious: 15%

Conservative Christian: 12%

Other religiously affiliated: 12%

**Salaries**

$10,000 – $15,000 less than public schools

**Schools: 35,000**

**Represent: 24% of all US schools**

**Educate: 9% of US students**

*Source: National Center for Education Statistics,*
*National Assessment of Educational Progress*

# Pros of Private Schools

Oversee their own curriculum and funding so they are not bound by government requirements.

No teaching license required with experience and expertise valued for hiring.

Entrance exam required for admittance with students showing they have the skills for success in academic studies.

Fewer and less severe discipline issues than public schools with schools able to expel students for misbehavior.

Students outperform public school students on practically every topic in standardized and college entry tests. (Source: National Assessment of Educational Progress NAEP, 2015 and 2016)

Smaller class size than public schools, making it easier for a teacher to monitor and support students' learning.

# Chapter Eight

# FAMILY MATTERS

Just before school started for all four of us, my children and I flew to visit family in Lake Tahoe. I had accepted the job offer at the Catholic school. With two weeks off between jobs, why not visit family in the place I considered my spiritual home? We fished for crawdads, swam at a state park, and hiked the Tahoe Rim Trail with its gorgeous views of the Sierra Nevada Mountains. Most importantly, we reconnected with extended family at my mom's mountain retreat in Incline Village.

At a happy hour on my mother's deck, my older brother Jeff scolded me for leaving journalism.

"But Jinge, you love writing for the newspaper," he said, using my childhood nickname. "You're one of the few people I know who likes her job."

"I can always return to journalism if I don't like teaching," I said, sitting next to him on the deck bench.

I viewed him as insightful, intelligent, and a good listener—even if he was sometimes bossy and unwavering in his opinions.

He shook his head. "That's sometimes tough to do."

He was my big brother, and believed that, as a little sister, I knew less than he did.

"Why? I've left jobs before," I said. "It hasn't been that hard to find another one."

"You're leaving the profession," he said, as he sipped from his glass of chardonnay. "You won't be a journalist anymore. Everyone will see you as a teacher. It's not going to be easy to switch back."

His words caught me by surprise. No one else had discouraged me from taking the plunge into teaching.

"I hope you're wrong," I said. "I don't know if I want to spend the rest of my life in teaching, but a couple of years might not be bad."

"You might get stuck there," he said, munching on mixed nuts. "Your heart is in journalism. Do you feel the same way about teaching?"

In only a few minutes, he pinpointed my misgivings about teaching.

"Not really," I said, sighing. "But I'm stressed at the newspaper. I don't have enough time with my kids. Their father is super busy with his career. He doesn't help as much as I'd like."

"The divorce is now finalized?" asked Jeff, nibbling on cheese and crackers.

I nodded. "That happened two months ago."

"It's not easy living with someone and raising kids together," he said. "But when Jane and I divorced, it was a big relief. I'm much happier now with Sandy—she's my soulmate."

"Someday, I'd like to remarry," I said. "With teaching, I might actually have time to look for someone."

"But will you be alright working with teenagers?" asked Jeff. "They're horrible."

"Since my kids aren't yet that age, I'm not sure what they're like," I said. "I guess I'll find out soon."

"I hated teaching," he said, a slight anger creeping into his voice. "Those kids were brats. They were so obnoxious. It was the worst. They never listened to me. They didn't respect adults. Jane and I had planned to teach overseas and do photography and art on the side. But I hated it so much that I never wanted to go in a classroom again."

"You were student teaching in a bad district," I said. "If you'd been at a better school, it might have been different."

We all remembered how mom had urged Jeff to finish that last college course, so that if he ever needed money, he could teach. He'd been adamant; he would never teach again. Sometimes I thought this was his best decision, since he ended up pursuing his calling as a photographer and visual artist. But for some years, this career choice had left him impoverished.

Jeff paused to drink more wine, thinking as he gazed at the pines and red firs dotting the property, the crystal blue lake partially hidden. "Maybe it will work out for you. But you might hate the kids as much as I did."

"They're girls at a Catholic school," I said. "How bad can they be? I'm sure the nuns keep them in line."

I expected these young women to be as disciplined as when I was a second grader in Saint Dominique, a Catholic school in

Morocco. There, I'd been afraid to act up, worried I'd be punished by the principal—or worse, God.

"Well, good luck," he said. "Maybe you'll like it and be happy, but you might regret your decision."

★ ★ ★

Back home, I sat cross-legged on a fluffy carpet in my family room, a half dozen French books surrounding me. That Labor Day weekend, I needed to prepare for my first week of teaching. In a composition notebook, I jotted down a plan for the first days of school:

1. Hand out textbooks.
2. Go over classroom rules.
3. Evaluate students' ability in French.

We would cover a dozen pages in the textbook, and they'd write a paragraph about themselves and say it to the class. By doing this, we would get to know each other. Was this overly ambitious?

To familiarize myself with vocabulary and grammar, I thumbed through the *Dis-Moi! Level 1* textbook, all very easy until I stumbled on the word "partitive." Why didn't I recognize this word? I panicked. A quick Google search confused me; a partitive was a noun or pronoun used in a partitive construction. What did that mean?

In *Essential French Grammar,* I searched the table of contents and index. Nothing on partitives. Genevieve would know the answer, but my pride stopped me from phoning her. After all, in college, I'd mastered French. I fingered through the grammar book, its smooth cover calming my nerves as I flipped through its pages once again.

Une vieille dame . . . *An old lady* . . . Elle la lui donne . . . Il faut que je fasse. *It was all coming back to me. I'd be okay.*

I took a deep breath. Forget partitives; no one would ask me about them. I needed to brush up on French authors by reading excerpts of Balzac and Voltaire. I'd first test myself to see how much I remembered. I didn't want one smarty-pants girl to know more about French literature than I did. Camus was an existentialist, who'd written *L'Etranger*. Voltaire was a philosopher, while Balzac must have been a Romantic, or maybe a realist. I had stuffed too much information in my brain to recall much else from these French intellectuals who had little relevance to my life now. After all, would Voltaire help me convince Emily to tidy up her room? Would Camus make it easier to handle Patrick's volatile temper? Would Balzac tell me how to become a well-loved teacher or find a romantic partner?

How well I remember my father discussing Balzac's *Père Goriot* with me. Dad, who'd read the book in his twenties, talked about a father's financial ruin and sacrifices to his egotistical daughters. Dad was like that, recalling all sorts of information until he got sick with cancer. What would Dad think of my leaving journalism, a profession he'd once considered before becoming a diplomat? He was so proud of me when I'd graduated from Columbia's journalism school and then landed a job at a newspaper. I recalled his words of advice: Find a profession that excites you with colleagues you enjoy. I doubted he'd approve of my becoming a teacher; like Jeff, he believed my heart belonged in journalism.

On the other hand, Mom was all for teaching. Her mother had taught kindergarten for several decades, a job that had brought her financial security after her divorce. Her ancestors, the Bennion and Merrill families, came from a long line of prominent Mormon educators in Utah and California. Mom viewed teaching as a noble, respected career.

I made a final attempt to discover the truth about partitives. In *La Grammaire à l'oeuvre*, my beat-up, go-to grammar book from UC Berkeley, I found it. It was used to describe uncountable nouns, translated as "some" or "any."

*Voulez-vous du beurre?* Do you want some butter? *Nous avons bu du vin rouge avec le diner.* We drank some red wine with dinner.

Wow, that was easy. Why had I stressed over it? French grammar wasn't complicated. Teaching was going to be a breeze; no need to worry or overthink it.

## Top Reasons to Teach

**You Impact the Future.**

"Teaching is a very noble profession that shapes the character, caliber, and future of an individual. If the people remember me as a good teacher, that will be the biggest honor for me."

—**A.P.J Abdul Kalam**, former President of India

"The youth of today are the leaders of tomorrow."

—**Nelson Mandela**, former president of South Africa

"A teacher affects eternity; he can never tell where his influence stops."

—**Henry Adams**, American historian and author

"If you're in a profession you don't like, come and teach, because you'll find meaning every day. You'll find you can change someone's life."

—**Dr. Jill Biden**, First Lady and college educator

"The task of the modern educator is not to cut down jungles, but to irrigate deserts."

—**C.S. Lewis**, British writer

"I touch the future. I teach."

—**Christa McAuliffe**, American teacher and astronaut

"Education is our passport to the future, for tomorrow belongs to the people who prepare for it today."

—**Malcolm X**, American minister and human rights activist

"The art of teaching is the art of assisting discovery."

—**Mark Van Doren**, American poet

**You're Needed.**

In February 2022, some 380,000 open jobs existed in schools and universities, the highest number of openings in the past decade. (Bureau of Labor Statistics)

Employment of high school teachers is projected to grow 5% from 2021 to 2031 and 4% for middle and elementary school teachers. (Bureau of Labor Statistics)

Special education, elementary, math, science, and world language are experiencing acute teacher shortages. (EdWeek Research Center Survey in 2022)

# Chapter Nine

# LA RENTRÉE

S weat trickled down my back as I surveyed the classroom to make sure it was ready for *la rentrée*, the much-anticipated first day of school. I had neatly arranged student desks and stored textbooks and dictionaries on a wooden bookshelf. The clock above the door watched over me, its hands predictably advancing—only twenty minutes until students entered.

I opened the windows, longing for a gust of wind to disperse the room's stagnant, hot air. No such luck. With a tissue, I wiped moisture off my face. On the blackboard, I quickly wrote the school's required prayer in French. Then I spoke it softly to achieve serenity—and make sure I knew its contents.

I clutched my marble composition notebook—the one with lesson plans and student rosters—as if it were a Bible with all the answers.

Breathing in deeply to calm my nerves, I paced the room. *Please, please, let the students be kind!* Through the open door, I heard muffled voices and laughter, and rushed to greet students.

Two girls in gray pleated skirts and white polo shirts stepped into the classroom, introducing themselves as Niamh and Maeve. Four other girls—Tori, Daluchi, Liz, and Katherine—followed in quick succession. That was my entire French 2, period 1 class. "*Bonjour, classe. Je m'appelle Madame Nelson. Quel jour sommes nous?*" I asked, standing near the blackboard. "*Qui peut écrire la date sur le tableau?*"

They stared at me blankly; no one understood that I wanted someone to write the date on the board. They fidgeted in their seats, looking trapped in the gray cinder block room, their faces shiny with perspiration. It seemed like they were not yet ready for full immersion.

When I wrote the date and my grading policy on the board, then handed out copies of the textbook, they looked relieved. "This is a continuation of *Dis-Moi*, which you used in French 1, right?" I asked.

The girls looked down, averting my gaze. "We didn't do much work last year," admitted Niamh, a brunette with a ballet dancer's body.

"Why not?" I asked.

"Mrs. Sachs got tired of teaching, so she talked about her experiences in France during the war," said Niamh, clearly the class leader.

"At first, it was interesting learning about Catholics hiding her from Nazis," added Maeve, an athletic-looking tenth grader. "But after a while, we got bored with her stories from childhood."

"She told us she didn't need the money," said Niamh. "Her husband worked in finance in New York City."

*Wow, were teenagers always this direct with adults? Perhaps they didn't have filters. How fortunate Madame Sachs was to have a rich husband who made it possible for her to work at a low-paying job.*

"This year, with me, you'll learn more French. Let's start by reading a dialogue."

Niamh, Tori, and Maeve immediately volunteered, but as they were reading, tears started flowing down Daluchi's face. What should I do in this type of situation with a young person I barely knew? It seemed unkind to ignore her sadness, yet did she want attention drawn to her by my intervening? I approached her, asking if she was okay and if she wanted to leave the classroom. She shook her head. "We can talk after class," I whispered, putting my arm around her strong shoulders.

Immediately the other students started comforting Daluchi, who sniffled, her eyes puffy.

"It's hard not knowing anyone," said Niamh. "You'll make friends soon."

"The first day is hard," said Maeve, offering her a tissue. "But we're nice. You'll like us."

"It takes time to get used to this place," said Liz, who looked scholarly in small round glasses. "Give it a few days and you'll see how fun it is here."

Daluchi dabbled her eyes with the tissue, her face still red. "I'm good now. You can continue with the lesson."

*What made this young woman cry? Did I say something that bothered her? Was her mother dying of cancer, or had her father lost his job? Was she being abused? I'd later ask the nuns about her background and how best to help her.*

Maeve inched her desk closer to Daluchi's, a caring gesture, whispering to her. I imagined she was offering solace to a new student.

"Let's do a pronunciation drill," I said. "We'll use our books. Open to page five." Next, to get students back on track, they did a pronunciation drill, repeating sentences about how they got to school. Daluchi mouthed the words, but her eyes looked sad, and I worried about her. I vowed to find out what had led her to cry.

Ten minutes before class ended, I gave them their first assignment of drawing a picture and writing sentences about a dream profession. Sister Lillian would display their pictures on the career bulletin board in the school's lobby for Back-to-School Night.

Students peppered me with questions: Could they use artwork from the Internet? What was the French word for designer, literary critic, and cook? Was it okay to write in the present tense? I handed out dictionaries and they searched for translations, enthusiastic about this project. I allowed a student to use the teacher's computer to research professions. Only Daluchi seemed lost, her head bent over a blank sheet of paper.

"I don't know what kind of job I want," she lamented.

"That's okay," I said, sitting down beside her. "Lots of teenagers don't. What do you do in your spare time?"

"I go to church."

"Perhaps you could be a pastor or youth group leader."

She looked troubled. "That doesn't sound good."

*I didn't ask her why she wasn't drawn to a religious profession; I wanted to know what excited her.* "What classes do you like at school?"

"Last year, my math teacher was cool."

Eventually, I convinced her to depict math-related professions, such as a statistician or accountant, though she was lukewarm about these jobs. I assured her that as a ninth grader she had years to figure out a career path and shouldn't feel anxious about her future.

The bell clanged, startling me. "I don't think I'll ever get used to that," I muttered under my breath. "Can't the nuns lower the volume?"

Tori walked by me. "You know it's right outside your door," she said with a smile. "Give it a month and you won't even notice it."

I laughed, a lightness entering my body as I realized I could be myself around these girls.

"Ciao," said Niamh, waving her hand.

I stopped Daluchi before she exited. "Is everything okay now?"

Daluchi hesitated a moment, her eyes darting around the room as if demons lurked in its corners. "This class is way too tough for me. I didn't understand anything you said in French."

*Really? That was it? Thank goodness I hadn't said anything to upset her, and her mother wasn't ill or her father jobless. She wasn't being mistreated at home.*

"Maybe you're just rusty after summer. Didn't you have French 1 in middle school?"

"After Christmas, they cancelled the class. I was at a public school in Trenton. The teacher was ill."

*Wow! I can't believe they hadn't hired a substitute teacher for the rest of the school year. No wonder she was lost.*

"Do you want to take French 1 instead? I teach that class sixth period."

"Yeah, I would . . ." she said, pausing to look at her schedule taped to a pink binder with flowers. "But I have gym then."

"Talk to Sister Mary Ann. She should be able to switch classes."

"I'll do that during lunch," said Daluchi, smiling. "Thank you, Madame Nelson."

From the second story window, I peered down at the lush fir trees and dirt walking paths on the school's spacious grounds; I had no desire to flee. All had gone well that first period. I'd helped a student, a girl who like me was new and finding her direction in a place where she didn't know the rules, expectations, or people. It wasn't easy to be the newbie—for either of us—and I was proud I'd known what to say to make her feel better. No student had talked back to me or refused to work. They were model students, listening to directions, caring about a fellow student, and working on their assignment. My brother Jeff was wrong about teaching. I was going to be fine at this school.

But how had my three kids managed without me that morning? I'd left forty-five minutes before them, missing my normal routine of handing out bag lunches, kissing them on their heads, and shooing them out the kitchen door.

"Did everyone get to school okay?" I texted Emily, my seventh grade daughter.

"I made it on the bus. How should I know what Patrick and Nicholas did?" replied Emily.

"Didn't they leave when you did?" I texted back.

"No, Mom, they didn't. They have only two blocks to walk."

At bedtime the night before, Nicholas had assured me that he'd get himself and Patrick to the elementary school on time. Patrick had promised to follow Nicky's instructions. They could handle this responsibility. But was it legal to leave such young children home alone, even for less than an hour? Did I have a choice? I couldn't be late to my first period class nor could I call my sons on the landline during class. My sons had refused to attend early morning day care, claiming it was for babies. I messaged my daughter saying we'd get her brothers cell phones at the mall that weekend. Then I could reach them anytime.

I momentarily thought about calling the elementary school to ask them about Nicholas and Patrick, but that would be weird. What kind of mom didn't know if her children had made it to school? I rationalized that the school would contact me if my boys were absent. I had to trust them to get to school on time.

They'd been thrilled about my new job, since it meant they would no longer spend afternoons with their elderly babysitter who'd gobbled down bologna and cheese sandwiches as she sat on the couch watching television, her smelly feet resting on the coffee table. The children had complained about her butter-laden potatoes and overcooked vegetables, and how they didn't feel safe when she drove them to soccer practice in her old station wagon. Mom would do a better job than her. She'd help them with homework, take them to practices, and cook healthy dinners—and love them more than any outsider would.

★ ★ ★

At 2:30 p.m. the last bell rang, and a dozen ninth graders left my classroom. A breeze drifted through the window, cooling the room as I sat down at my desk to review the next day's lesson. Cicadas buzzed in the distance, the sanitized smell of newly cleaned floors dissipating.

"Can I talk to you a minute?" said Daluchi, walking into the room.

"Of course."

"I've switched to French 1," she announced, grinning. "I'll be in your sixth period class tomorrow."

"That's good news," I said. "You'll be happier there."

She smiled broadly. "I'll understand what's going on."

Feeling proud I had helped someone that day, I watched Daluchi slip away into the quiet hallway. Not one girl had asked me to explain Camus or Voltaire or fancy words only intellectuals understood. The girls, even in the Advanced Placement class, stumbled on French words, failing to understand me when I talked at a normal pace. My French skills were more than adequate to teach here; students less intimidating and kinder than I had expected. My friends had been right: I had the knowledge and personality to teach French. I was off to a great start.

First Days
of School

### Show Confidence

You know what you're doing—even if you're nervous or insecure.

### Establish Rules

My cardinal rule: Respect each other, the teacher, the classroom, and oneself.

### Set Goals

Determine goals for students as individuals and a class. Post class objectives daily to achieve these goals.

### Get to Know Students

Learn their names quickly. Identify an interest in each of your students.

### Access Technology

Some students need help logging on to laptops and digital platforms.

### Discuss Grades

Explain types of assignments, point values, due dates, and late policy.

## Chapter Ten

# A BLESSED TIME

What a change of heart I had those three years teaching at the Catholic school! I felt at peace in the nuns' presence, supported by a community that valued education. The girls and I enjoyed each other's company as we worked on French activities, exercises, and projects. I could be myself around these young people, as we respected each other. They forgave my occasional mistakes, such as mixing up the names of students and scolding a class for being lazy. The weekly religious services and fall spiritual retreat at the shore relaxed me, the stress of meeting journalism deadlines disappearing. I felt at ease speaking French with the girls as I pushed them to work hard. They didn't complain assignments and tests were too demanding; instead, they buckled down and got the work done and gradually learned French. They made my job easy. Each year, I was ecstatic when they showed their appreciation by giving me small Christmas gifts like homemade cookies, decorative candles, and books on Provence and Paris. I received end-of-year notes with hearts drawn next to words of praise for a fun, fulfilling year. How touching were their words and actions! I sent them thank you cards, telling them how special they were and wishing them a relaxing summer.

To satisfy my creative urges, I started writing stories during lunch. I couldn't completely leave writing! More importantly, I spent ample time with my own kids. In the afternoon I arrived home with enough energy to devote my full attention to parenting. I talked to my children about their day, made sure they did chores, and guided them in making right decisions. I loved them and wanted them to grow up to be confident, caring adults. Certainly, they noticed I was more present in their lives, seeing me as a calmer, more balanced mom than the frazzled, overworked person I had been as a reporter.

As my mother once had, I showed them how to celebrate important holidays as part of a family. For Halloween we carved pumpkins together, hung skeletons and witches on our home's porch, and went trick-or-treating. For Christmas we retrieved a dozen boxes from the basement to decorate the house with angels, snowmen, a Nativity scene, and an eight-foot Christmas tree. The kids helped in the holiday preparations, and I had the stamina to finish the job when they inevitably lost interest. We raked leaves on Thanksgiving morning while the turkey roasted in the oven, the boys competing to make the biggest piles. We did just fine without a man in the house.

Summer meant spending leisurely days at a local pool, taking ten-day trips to Lake Tahoe, and reading books from the town's library. The children got together with their neighborhood friends, rode bikes, and played indoor and outdoor games. I followed my mother's model on how to raise children: Always show them love, listen to them, and accept that they might occasionally stumble on the path to adulthood. I was proud of creating a healthy home environment that contributed to a normal childhood for my children.

After Labor Day, my kids and I reestablished our daily routine: 6:30 a.m.: wake-up; 7:05 a.m.: school bus arrival; 3:30 p.m.: homework, sport practices; 6 p.m.: dinner; 10 p.m.: lights out.

After a long summer together, it was time for more structured days. Every other weekend Henrik took the children, leaving me time to explore occasional dating.

That first year, Mitchell from the business journal sent me a letter on scented stationery, suggesting we get together. I agreed to meet him, and our friendship eventually blossomed into a romance that almost led to marriage. For Valentine's Day, Mitchell sent me a gorgeous bouquet of red roses, labeled "From your secret admirer." My students had been too polite to ask who'd sent the flowers, but they guessed it was from Madame's boyfriend. He continued to lavish me with gifts: Cheval Sauvage, his favorite California wine, Lindt chocolate, and flowers—long after we were a couple. He won over my two sons by treating them to all the candy they could dream of and roughhousing with them. But when my daughter heard him swear one day, she no longer wanted him in our lives.

Nonetheless, after romantic getaways in Paris and Lake Tahoe, Mitchell suggested we move to one of those two places. We could buy a house or rent an apartment, where we'd enjoy wine, writing and romance—and in Tahoe, cross-country skiing and hiking.

Mitchell loved my family and was fascinated by my brother Jeff's yearly ritual of attending Burning Man, a gathering of unconventional artists in the Black Rock desert of Nevada. On a trip to Washington, DC, Mitchell, a father of two, had entertained my children when they got bored visiting museums. He played tag with them outside, told jokes and amusing stories, and swung them around. I could see us blending our families together but something in my heart told me he wasn't The One.

I shared my thoughts about Mitchell with Tess, my new friend at the Catholic school, who'd survived a messy divorce. I wasn't aware of her heart-wrenching story until she handed me a copy of her book, *Rescued,* with a cover photo of her with her two children. After their breakup, Tess had moved back to the United States from Iran. She had custody of the children, but that didn't prevent her Iranian husband from abducting them, claiming she would never see them again. In hindsight, my divorce was simple: no kidnapped children, no $200,000 bribes, no spousal abuse. She had remarried and eventually rescued the children and returned them to America. The story, written by a ghostwriter, opened up my eyes to the challenges some women face after a breakup of a marriage, and how I must always remember how some students might have family secrets that could explain different behaviors.

Over lunches in the counseling office Tess provided dating advice, remarking how happy I was with Mitchell in my life while questioning why I should rush to remarry. I didn't need to overthink matters. Just enjoy his company. Wasn't it great, she said, that as a father himself, he could relate to my situation?

We also chatted about school matters. With enrollment numbers down my second year, the nuns fretted about keeping the school open, and we asked ourselves if someday our jobs would be eliminated. Frankly, I enjoyed the office gossip—if remarks weren't malicious or hurtful— and feeling part of a community that kept tabs on each other.

The only downside to my job teaching at Sacred Heart was its low salary. Once child support and alimony ended when the children finished college, I'd need a higher paying job. I couldn't discount doubling my salary by working at a public school, even if the nuns would resent me for leaving. So, with hesitation during my second year, I started Alternate Route, the process of state certification for those without a degree in education. Over eighteen months I took several graduate-level classes, attended a course on the realities of teaching, and passed several proficiency exams. Sacred Heart's physics teacher Les agreed to mentor me, observing my afternoon French class twice a week. Occasionally he fell asleep, later claiming it had nothing to do with my teaching. But the girls were all wide awake, the lessons entertaining enough for them. I'd completely adjusted to working with teenagers, feeling at ease in the classroom. I was a success here, so why wouldn't it be the same at a public school?

Two weeks before summer vacation, I landed what I believed to be the perfect public school teaching job with a robust salary, decent retirement benefits, and a manageable commuting distance. I felt prepared to work at Northern School District after completing the Alternate Route training program. Every Monday evening, at a local university, I had learned about problems public school teachers faced and ways to bring a classroom under control. I had discounted the advice, thinking that these problems wouldn't apply to me. Instead, I believed I could suppress students' negative attitudes, disrespect, and laziness by just being myself—and teaching using methods and techniques like the ones I had developed at Sacred Heart.

I dreaded telling the sisters I would not be returning in the fall. After all, I'd succeeded at this school with staff, students and parents appreciating my dedication. I'd made a difference in my students' lives. In the embrace of the sisters, I'd found an inner peace. Through this job, I had newfound freedoms to make my own family a priority in my life.

As I entered the meeting room, Sisters Lillian, Mary Ann, and Agnes rose from metal chairs tucked under a rectangular table. They shook my hand, still welcoming me into the flock. June's heat seeped into the room.

"We're uncertain why you want to leave us," said Sister Mary Ann, the down-to-earth principal. "Hasn't this school become your second home?"

I squirmed in a student chair. "Yes, you've treated me like family," I said. "But I need a job with a higher salary. Northern offers that."

Sister Lillian leaned forward in her chair as if preparing to tell a secret. "Public schools don't have the same caliber of students as we do. You might have problems with attitude. The kids won't respect you. Are you sure you want to leave our community?"

*She'd said these same words at my first interview almost three years earlier. But certainly now I was prepared to tackle these challenges.*

"I won't be able to get by on the salary here," I said. "My ex-husband helps me now, but the alimony payments will eventually end."

No need to mention that Northern offered a pension plan and generous health care package.

"You could stay in the little house near the convent," said Sister Mary Ann. "You wouldn't need to pay rent. You know the one I'm talking about?"

I nodded. The history teacher had lived in the two-bedroom house before getting married and finding a job elsewhere.

"It's very kind of you to offer the house. But my kids like where we live. They don't want to leave their school."

"Your daughter could go to school here," suggested Sister Mary Ann.

After a visit to the school, Emily had rejected the idea of

attending, disliking its smallness and antiquated technology. "But my sons can't go here," I said.

At that point, I wanted to separate my private and professional lives. Living on the grounds of the campus would make that difficult.

"You haven't been here that long," said Sister Mary Ann, almost begging. "Couldn't you stay another year?

"Northern needs someone in September," I said. "They won't let me defer it."

The nuns lowered their eyes, hands folded as if in prayer—and remained silent. I had betrayed them. I blabbered on about how much I loved the school, then suggested that Karin, who had interviewed me, could replace me.

"We'd heard rumors you might leave, so we made inquiries into her situation," said Sister Lillian. "She was flattered we asked her, but said no. She wants to spend more time with her children for a few more years."

She pursed her lips, challenging me to reconsider my decision. But I'd already committed to Northern.

"There will be people looking to teach French," I said. "Perhaps someone like me who's new to the profession, or like Les who's retired from teaching and wants extra income."

"It's hard to find dedicated, hardworking people," said Sister Lillian.

Sister Mary Ann softened. "We would like to pay you more, but if we did that, we'd have to do it for all the staff. We don't have the funds for that."

"It would be different if I were married," I said. "Then money wouldn't be as important."

Finally Sister Lillian's face lit up. "Certainly that will happen, won't it?"

*Had they heard about Mitchell?*

"I can't count on getting married," I said.

How I wish I could have told them I was engaged, ready to settle down with Mitchell and create a future together as we merged two families. Instead, several months earlier, I had broken up with him.

"Well, it seems we aren't going to convince you to stay," said Sister Mary Ann. "Just be aware that you're taking the wrong path. It's going to be tough for you. You're not used to disgruntled young people who treat adults poorly. You will regret your decision."

*Wow, I felt as if they were condemning me to purgatory.*

"I believe I'm prepared to teach at a public school," I said. "But I'll miss everyone here. You've been so kind to me."

We stood. With a deep sigh, I looked down as each of the sisters somberly filed out of the room without the usual farewells. They didn't bless me for my upcoming journey or thank me for three years of service. They left without shaking my hand. I felt rejected.

Yet a few months later, I began to see the painful truths of Sister Mary Ann's prophesy.

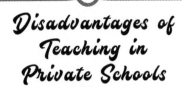

# Disadvantages of Teaching in Private Schools

Salaries are 30% less than at public schools with an average annual salary of $46,400 versus $61,600 at public schools. (Source: National Center for Education Statistics)

Teachers have non-teaching duties such as coaching a sport, running a club, and overseeing a dorm, and do not receive extra pay.

No strong union that offers advice and support for difficulties at work.

Offers limited services and resources for special needs students.

May be considered elitist with many well-off students and few poor students attending.

# Chapter Eleven

## A MODEL LESSON

After several months at Northern, I felt like a complete failure. I couldn't control my students, my supervisor had given me a scathing first evaluation, and I was beginning to hate teenagers. I dreaded entering the classroom. Every day I thought about quitting, but my colleague Nabila encouraged me to stay, saying students would warm up to me. All I needed to do was implement strategies she used. I agreed to observe one of her classes; maybe by imitating Nabila I could succeed in my classroom.

One November morning I walked into Nabila's French 2 class, determined to discover the secrets to her success. In a notebook tucked in my Vera Bradley book bag, I planned to write down improvement strategies. I expected Nabila to dazzle students with her knowledge and enthusiasm for her subject matter, keep in line every student, and speak at least 80% of the time in French. I was curious about what she'd do to make sleepy and lazy students work. Certainly she'd include an informal assessment and scold in French the students who misbehaved. Would she end class early given that it was the period before lunch when students thought more about food than French?

I marveled at how happy Nabila was that day, as if the classroom were her favorite place to be. She sported her signature teacher's garb: a flared, pink and yellow Ann Taylor skirt and sweater set and black pumps. She greeted smiling students at the door, then casually conversed with them in French as she noted on her clipboard which students were absent. No one muttered how they hated the class or how bored they expected themselves to be. She elegantly moved to the front of the class where all eyes were on her as she discussed the day's topic: daily routine and objects used for personal hygiene. The essential question was written on the board: How does the daily routine of French teens differ from American teens? Wow, it was the same lesson that Nabila had helped me design for my observation.

Seconds after the bell rang, Nabila told students to retrieve the dialogue she had handed out the previous day. Students rummaged through their backpacks. Only a few couldn't find theirs, and Nabila immediately handed them another copy. They thanked her, and the lesson resumed without delay. There were no stragglers.

*Boy, was she organized! Evidently I hadn't learned the importance of getting down to business as soon as class started. In the next SOS meeting, I want to know about strategies to make this work.*

Northern required first-year teachers to attend an SOS program, which aimed to aid and retain teachers by offering advice and support in monthly meetings. Our group of fifteen teachers had already met briefly just before school started. In a notebook provided by the SOS program, I wrote down takeaways:

* ★ Photocopy extra handouts for students who misplace theirs.
* ★ Don't comment on why they can't find the handout.
* ★ Move on quickly to teach the lesson.
* ★ Don't waste time.

Nabila asked for volunteers to read a dialogue about a brother and sister getting ready for school. A sea of hands shot up. "*C'est bien que vous participez,*" announced Nabila, beaming. "*C'est le tour de Brad and Angie aujourd'hui.*"

*Wow, what great participation—and Brad and Angie look happy she picked them!*

Brad, a lanky teen with disheveled hair, and Angie, a heavy-set girl with wistful blue eyes, got up from seats that had been arranged in a horseshoe configuration, and walked to the board. In my notebook, I penned another takeaway:

* ★ Change my classroom seating arrangement from rows to a horseshoe. Then I will easily see everyone; no one can hide in the back.

Brad and Angie read the dialogue, projecting loud enough for all to hear. Students listened attentively, interested in seeing how their peers fared in the spotlight. Nabila occasionally stopped Brad and Angie to check that everyone understood key vocabulary and grammar points, translating into English words like *se reveiller* (to wake up), *se lever* (to get up), and *se coucher* (to go to bed). She encouraged students to take notes so they could refer to them when answering comprehension questions. Some complied, others appeared too drained to make the effort. Nabila didn't insist. Students clapped after Brad and Angie finished the dialogue; one boy even high-fived Brad as he retreated to his seat, grinning.

"*Maintenant répondez aux questions au verso du papier*," announced Nabila, showing them the backside of the dialogue's paper. "*Je vais projeter le dialogue sur le SmartBoard. Vous pouvez travailler avec un partenaire ou seule.*"

A handful of students moved to different seats to work with friends, while others started talking to the person next to them. One muttered she didn't understand the assignment. "We just have to answer the comprehension questions," a serious-looking boy said. "You can work alone or with a partner."

I added key points to my SOS notebook:

* It's okay to let students choose their own partners to complete tasks.
* Let students sometimes take charge of their learning.
* If they don't like taking notes, don't require them to do so.

As students worked, Nabila casually roamed around the room, a flowery skirt clinging to her curvaceous figure, chattering in French about her daily routine. I felt as if she were taking a stroll with friends along the Boulevard Champs Elysees, enjoying the teens around her. She stopped to help students who'd raised their hand. Students welcomed the individual attention, thanking her for her assistance. One girl asked in French to use the bathroom, and Nabila gave her a pass. A boy started doing math homework—Nabila told him firmly to put the notebook under his desk. She laughed at a student's joke. Her ease and confidence made it look as if she were born to teach.

"*Finissez dans cinq minutes*," she announced, looking at the clock. "*On va corriger les questions*."

Only fifteen minutes were left in the period—and they couldn't be wasted. Nabila told students to exchange papers, then she called on two people to ask and answer the question, picking students using popsicle sticks written with their names.

*Those colored popsicle sticks are so cool! I need to use them in my class.*

In my notebook, I wrote:

★ Make popsicle sticks with students' names on them to use in speaking assignments. Give students points if they answer a question when their popsicle stick is picked. Brilliant idea!

After most students had asked or answered a question, Nabila praised them for their efforts, then assigned homework of writing four sentences about their daily routine. She ended the lesson three minutes early. Students started packing up their backpacks, congregating around the door. Was this allowed?

"*Bon travail*," she said, as they exited. "*A demain*."

Students marched out of the room in an orderly line. Several asked about the homework. No one moaned about the workload.

The lesson had flowed smoothly, as if the whole class had been leisurely cruising down a slow, deep river. Nabila's students hadn't interrupted her. They occasionally whispered to each other, but they did this sparingly and with obvious respect for their teacher. She never got annoyed, effortlessly controlling a group of teenagers.

"What a great lesson," I said, as Nabila and I left the classroom. "You make teaching look so easy."

"Remember I've been here six years. I know the kids and what administrators expect from us," said Nabila, walking toward the lunchroom. "You'll get it. It just takes a while."

"I hope so," I said. "I took notes to help me remember what to do."

Nabila chuckled. "That's what I like about you, Jen. You're a star pupil."

"With you, I am. I'm not sure I'm that way with my own students," I said. "By the way, you ended the lesson early. Can you do that?"

"Never cram too much into a lesson," she said. "Students need time to absorb the material. Besides, just before lunch, they're hungry and can't concentrate."

I bet Leslie would have crucified me if I'd done that. "I saw how some of them were starting their homework. So it's not like they were all wasting time."

Nabila nodded. "Leslie doesn't like us giving homework very often, but I think it's needed to get through the curriculum."

I'd given up on assigning homework in my French 2 class. Only a few people did it, and those who got zeros didn't seem to care. Besides, Leslie hated it, and I certainly wanted to try to please her.

"I picked up some tips from you, so maybe I won't get fired this year."

Nabila laughed. "That won't happen. You have months to improve. Stop being so hard on yourself. You know kids have different learning styles, right?" Nabila asked.

In my teacher training program, we briefly talked about the primary learning styles: auditory, visual, analytical, verbal, and kinesthetic, though I hadn't emphasized them in my lesson plans. I was having a tough time on other issues, mainly classroom management, the key to all success.

Nabila recommended I use pictures for visual learners, music and listening exercises for auditory ones, movement for kinesthetic ones, reading for analytical ones, and speaking for verbal ones.

"It's not that complicated if you just do a reading, writing, listening, and speaking activity every day in class," she said. "Also, occasionally tell them in French to stand up and stretch and move around the classroom so they don't get antsy in their seats."

I looked at her in amazement. Why hadn't I learned to structure my lessons this way during Alternate Route? During that course, I had learned how to write a lesson plan using anticipatory sets, objectives, guided practice, checking for understanding, and exit tickets. Teachers of all subject matters were expected to follow this model. I found the pedagogical jargon too complicated. Now Nabila was showing me an easier, simpler, and more effective way to teach.

"I can put all these different activities into my lesson," I said. "It's a good structure to follow."

The Alternate Route program had focused on strategies to make students learn, control misbehavior, and engage them in the subject matter. I'd been lectured about how to deal with disruptive, unmotivated students during this technological age when computers and cell phones provided answers to most—if not all—questions. Students were questioning if they needed to memorize historical facts, learn a foreign language, or remember a math formula when with a few clicks with their mouse they'd find the answer. Regrettably, I'd discounted key advice from this program, believing it didn't apply to me.

Nabila encouraged me to incorporate collaborative activities into every lesson. Kids could work with a partner or in a small group, where the learning environment is more relaxed and less solitary. The classroom would evolve into a hub of activity and energy in which students took charge of their learning, and the teacher was no longer the center of attention.

"We're just facilitators in the classroom," said Nabila. "We plan the activities—and you must get ones that kids like—but then it's up to them to get the work done and show they've learned the material."

My image of the ideal classroom had to change. I'd always pictured it as a center of scholarly pursuits in which students sat in rows in a library-esque atmosphere where discussion was discouraged, individual achievement rewarded, and educators revered. Students consulted textbooks daily and always completed homework. Now, educational pedagogy acknowledged that students learned in different ways, so I needed to get with the program and embrace new practices such as collaborative learning and differentiated instruction. It was time I let go of the dated model I grew up with, one that favored analytical and solitary learners.

Nabila made me hopeful that all I had to do was keep working at it. In my classroom, I'd try to imitate Nabila's bubbly personality and confidence while implementing strategies listed in my SOS notebook. I had to start liking my students. They drove me nuts with their laziness, complaints, and disinterest. Would they ever see me as kind and caring the way my Sacred Heart students had seen me? Was it possible to become likable this late in the school year? I would try my best to change the dynamics in my class.

The Catholic school students had respected me, and certainly with Nabila's help, I now hoped some of these students would begin to like me as well. It wasn't only Nabila who was watching over me at Northern.

★ ★ ★

Mrs. Dawkins, one of the vice principals at the middle school, approached me on a dark November morning after I'd signed in. The trim, thirty-something woman with a navy-blue suit and high-heeled pumps ushered me into her office. We'd become friends earlier in the fall after we bonded about how we'd both been English majors in college.

"I hear one of your classes is giving you problems," she said.

*How quickly bad news travels!*

"Yes, at the high school," I said, almost ashamed.

"Look, if you don't mind, I could observe that class. Don't worry. It won't be part of your evaluation. I'll make comments on what I see. Then we'll talk about how to turnaround the class."

I hated observations—particularly after Leslie's scathing report. Yet I trusted Mrs. Dawkins, who was kindly offering her services to help me improve.

"That would be great," I said. "Tell me when you're coming. I'll be prepared."

*Best States for Veteran Teachers*

(Ranked by top salaries)

1.  District of Columbia — $116,408

2.  California — $98,616

3.  New York — $94,541

4.  Connecticut — $94,294

5.  Washington — $95,006

6.  Maryland — *$93,262

7.  Massachusetts — *$93,262

8.  New Jersey — $93,035

9.  Hawaii — $88,839

10. Rhode Island — $87,637

*Tied for 6th place

*Source: National Education Association (NEA) 2019-2020 Teacher Salary Benchmark report.*

**Worst States for Veteran Teachers**

(Ranked by top salaries)

1. Arkansas — $53,780
2. Missouri — $56,275
3. Oklahoma — $57,013
4. Louisiana — $57,620
5. Idaho — $58,177
6. Kansas — $59,840
7. North Dakota — $61,316
8. Florida — $61,873
9. Kentucky — $62,706
10. North Carolina — $63,227

*Source: National Education Association (NEA)*
*2019-2020 Teacher Salary Benchmark report.*

# Chapter Twelve

## MY MISSION

It was going to be a great day—if not week—at Northern. By becoming more like Nabila Sherif, I would change my students' attitude toward me. I would relax in class, speak French, and make learning fun. Most importantly, I would start liking the students.

That weekend, to prepare for my transformation, I consulted my SOS notebook, making sure every lesson included a speaking, listening, writing, and reading activity—and an informal assessment. I created a seating chart—a horseshoe formation one—making sure students were not sitting close to friends. Not an easy task since ideally, I would have paired stronger students with weaker ones, but only Stephanie and Elizabeth seemed to understand much French. I did my best, considering students' work ethic and personality, though I expected students to object to working with someone they didn't know well. *Tant pis!*

I spent hours scouring the Internet for entertaining YouTube videos and readings on daily chores; developing handouts for listening and writing activities; and retrieving sponges, detergents, and a wisp broom from my utility closet to bring to class. Certainly, students would love seeing common household items, and wouldn't object to saying what these items were used for.

I meticulously planned the pacing of each activity. The key was not moving too fast or too slow through a lesson. Too fast, they were confused. Too slow, they were bored. Variety was essential—and organization a must.

For each day's lesson, I penned the following structure, varying the order of activities and including details about each one:

- ★ Do Now: (2-3 minutes)
- ★ Viewing (6-10 minutes)
- ★ Writing: (6-10 minutes)
- ★ Speaking/listening: (10-12 minutes)
- ★ Reading: (5-10 minutes)
- ★ Exit Ticket: (2-3 minutes)

By Sunday evening, I had five model lessons that looked great—at least on paper. How proud I felt of my plan for the upcoming week, and a little excited about implementing it with the Dirty Dozen, those spirited rascals I had to train to like French class. We were on a mission together—not to assassinate Nazis during World War II in a French chateau as in the *Dirty Dozen* movie, but to make the classroom a place conducive to learning. Certainly, if Major Reisman could succeed in working with rapists, murderers, and criminals on a dangerous assignment, I could handle changing the attitude of twelve middle-class teenagers, making them respect and work hard for me.

Nevertheless, I was anxious to know if I could ever be their commander. I thought about rewatching *Dirty Dozen* to see what strategies Reisman used to make his group respect him, but how much did criminals who were promised commuted sentences in return for success have in common with a bunch of high schoolers from small farming towns?

★ ★ ★

That Monday afternoon in late October, armed with my stellar lesson plans, I entered the classroom with a new mindset. I'd conquer this bunch, no matter what battles lay ahead. I expected struggles, particularly in the beginning when I challenged their authority. But eventually I'd evolve into their well-liked commander-in-chief.

I started class by telling students to find their new seat. "*Trouvez l'etiquette avec ton nom,*" I said, waving a sticky note with a name on it.

Michael accused me of forgetting he hadn't learned any French. Amanda and Meghan insisted students had a right to sit wherever they wanted. Chloe and Sara were more engrossed in their conversation than looking for their name tags. Only Aravind and Elizabeth obediently found their seats.

I glanced at my watch. Five minutes had elapsed—and still no student was working. What would Nabila do in this situation? Ignore the disorder? Start the lesson above their chattiness? Stare at them for minutes until the situation became so awkward that kids stopped talking? Scold them for wasting time? Over the past seven weeks, I'd used these strategies, but not one of them guaranteed order.

Instead, I'd show them an entertaining video about two brothers joking around as they did chores, making more of a mess while tidying up. This would quiet them down. "*Voila un fichier pour la video,*" I said, putting the video's handout on their desks.

I was besieged with a barrage of "I don't understand what you're saying," "What's this handout for?" and "What's going on with Madame today? She's weird."

Ignoring their outcry I started the video, and for a few minutes they were entertained by Abdou and Mohammed doing chores in a Parisian apartment. I breathed a sigh of relief. Finally, they were enjoying themselves in my class. I was on a roll.

Occasionally I stopped the video, asking them what chores the boys were doing. Only Stephanie responded. Not good. I needed everyone to participate. The handout would solve my problems. The film ended, and students commented in English on Abdou and Mohammed's failure to tidy up their apartment. "What a lame movie! No one cleans like that," "My mom would have grounded me if I'd done what those dudes did," and "Those French guys were hot."

Well, they were engaged. Now I had to get them to speak French. I encouraged them to look at the questions on the Smart-Board. Instead, they discussed in English how their families did chores at home. Only Stephanie finished the worksheet quickly. Several students asked to copy it. "*Mais vous ne pouvez pas faire cela,*" I scolded them. "*Vous n'allez pas appendre ni recevoir des points.*"

Stephanie translated what I said to the class. "She doesn't like it when you copy my paper. You're not going to get any points."

With that, they stopped copying—a plus—but then complained the handout was too hard. I told them to form groups to finish it; most students had copied enough answers to make the informal assessment invalid. I wouldn't give them points for cheating. But we'd go over the answers and then move on. At least they enjoyed the video. That was positive.

From a big plastic bin I pulled out a dish rag, dustpan and brush, Tide detergent, and Murphy's oil soap. Students looked on with interest. As I anticipated, they voiced their opinions: "My mom uses that stuff to clean floors," "That cloth is disgusting," and "What's that brush for?"

They were drawn to the lesson—and I was thankful for that—

but how could I harness that energy into speaking or writing French? I told them to take notes on the words on the board. Some complied; most did not.

I projected French verbs used for cleaning and asked them to repeat the words after me. Several participated, but most continued to talk among themselves about cleaning practices at home. In hindsight, I should have gotten angry at them—in a managed, controlled way—and told them in French to start working. They needed to know when I was disappointed in them, as well as when I was pleased with their efforts.

I hadn't yet learned how to show restrained anger in the classroom. I didn't feel I could yell at them, or send them to the principal's office, or write them up for defiance. I'd already emailed several parents about their child's misbehavior, but that hadn't resulted in much change. Although the students' actions hadn't required disciplinarian action, their disrespect was making it very difficult to work with them. I didn't like them, and that was suicidal for a teacher. In my class, power was gradually shifting from teacher to student—and I had to stop it soon. If they became the leaders of the class, the result would be anarchy.

I ended the class four minutes early—per Nabila's instructions. In the grade portal, only three students got credit for the speaking assignment; the rest got a zero. Maybe the next day, they'd start working to get points. I felt proud of the lesson—and my delivery of it—though the students' behavior hadn't improved. *Give it time*, I thought to myself. They'd come around. I just had to be patient—and plan structured, engaging lessons with an informal assessment. I had to always show I cared about them—and perhaps eventually we would start to like each other more.

★ ★ ★

The next day, before class started, Amanda and Meghan confronted me. Why had I given them a zero for the assignment on chores? I explained they hadn't spoken in French. Could they do it again? I didn't want students to realize that zeros could easily be converted into points if they just asked Madame for a second chance. Yet I wanted them to learn—and see me as a caring teacher. "Okay, ask and answer a question about what chores you do. I'll give you partial credit."

They beamed—and did the work. Several others who witnessed the interaction piped in that they too wanted to redo the assignment. It wasn't fair that two girls were allowed a retake, and others weren't. Well, that did it. We spent a good twenty minutes on the previous day's assignment—and all students received some points. I announced this was a one-time exception. Students had to complete work when it was due. Did they understand? They half-heartedly nodded. They weren't going to control the classroom on day #2 of that transformative week.

That Tuesday, I again got down to business. I sported a cute Ann Taylor skirt with a matching brown sweater set—a replica of Nabila's. Sara and Chloe commented on how I looked good in the outfit, and I thanked them.

I announced we'd start by reviewing the vocabulary of household cleaning products on my desk. One person would say in French what the item was, and the other, what it was used for. I urged them to consult their notes from the previous day, then pulled out the colored popsicle sticks and called on two students to start. Students brazenly critiqued my new educational strategies. "Madame, where did you get those sticks? Walmart?" "What color is mine? I don't like yellow, so it better not be yellow," and "What are we using those for?"

I had their attention—now to capitalize on that. I grabbed the rag and waved it in the air: "*C'est un chiffon. On l'utilise pour nettoyer.*" Then I wrote those sentences on the board as a model to follow.

"I don't have notes," said Aravind. "Does anyone else?" A cacophony of voices uttered no.

"We can't do this," said Michael. "You taught us nothing yesterday."

My face flushed red. Really? I'd busted my butt giving them information they needed to succeed, and they'd decided to ignore it. Didn't Michael realize that to learn he had to work? I explicitly told students to take notes the previous day. I refused to always give them handouts— writing helped them remember words.

Students should be held accountable. If they stopped being lazy, they all could learn. But teenagers preferred to take it easy. And in this case, the kids still resented my predecessor's low expectations of them.

"*Bon, voila les mots qu'on a étudiés,*" I said, writing the words on the board. "*Ecrivez les mots sur un papier.*"

Some objected, saying it was too much work or they didn't like to write. One asked if she could take a picture of the words using her cell phone. Cell phones were banned in class, I reminded her. Twenty minutes later, everyone was done. I deemed this an informal assessment. I ended class by telling them to review the words on their paper. They might have a pop quiz the next day.

Bad idea. Kids complained that wasn't enough time to learn ten new vocabulary words. Could it be an open note quiz? They hadn't learned any French the previous year—and they had work for other classes. The bell rang, saving me from lecturing them on how they should study every night and stop whining.

The next day, I dropped the pop quiz—and only Stephanie commented on that. They were right in that they needed days to master material, and that's what we'd do the rest of the week. Day

#3 we read a dialogue together—they each got a photocopied handout from the textbook, so no need to take notes. Then, with a partner, they answered comprehension questions on a piece of paper. As usual, they complained that the dialogue was too difficult. What did *faire la lessive, tondre la pelouse* and *arroser les plantes* mean? The dialogue was boring—no one liked doing chores, so why were these French teens not complaining? They weren't normal kids. They were prissy. Wow, couldn't my students stop with the commentaries? This was a hard crowd to please. They weren't interested in textbook activities used in classrooms nationwide. Technology might work, though I wasn't great at educational software.

How could I ever dream of winning them over?

I collected their papers. Three earned all four points for completing all questions in French, five received partial credit, and three got a zero. Most students had done the work—progress of some sort—but I was disappointed that 100% hadn't gotten full credit since we'd gone over the answers. What was wrong with my three failing students? Why weren't they motivated by grades?

Day #4 proved to be the same as the previous three days. Students talked during lessons and grumbled about completing work. Yet all scrambled to hand in the one activity I'd grade—even the three indolent ones—which made me feel I was making some progress. They said they weren't ready for a quiz on the material on Friday. How many days did it take for them to learn ten new vocabulary words? I agreed to postpone the quiz until Monday and do a review on Friday. Students would have two extra days to study to master the material—or so I hoped.

Day #5. It was time they took charge of their own study habits by reviewing for the quiz. I was drained from teaching four days, still not making as much progress earning their respect as I wanted. I wrote on the board what they were to study. They had the whole period to review—alone or with a partner—and I was there to help them. "So, it's not fun Friday?" asked Meghan. "Let's do a game to review?"

We'd played Jeopardy before, but that had ended in disaster. I wasn't yet ready to revisit it. Once I got control of the class, we'd do it. What was wrong with having a whole period to study? I asked them. Then, for the first time all week, I sat down at my desk. How nice it was to relax a few minutes and see several students diligently studying. Amanda and Meghan were goofing off and Michael was napping—and I reluctantly got up, urging them to study and not to waste class time. I was beat. It was now up to them to learn the material. They assured me they would study at home; I doubted they would.

That weekend, I again aimed to plan inspirational lessons, but the students had sapped my enthusiasm for creativity. It wasn't working for me to continue comparing them to the girls at Sacred Heart. I felt demoralized, questioning if I had what it took to turn around this group of students. I was doing okay—not great— with my middle school students—a bright spot—so replicating what I did there might work. I kept telling myself I just needed to continue to teach with reasonable expectations for my Dirty Dozen. Be positive. Be energetic. Don't lose my cool. The following week would be better, wouldn't it?

It was not.

I couldn't understand their work ethic. My mother's family embraced educators: my great uncle had taught university, and my grandmother, after a divorce, had been a kindergarten teacher. I was raised to value curiosity, education, and knowledge. Why couldn't my students understand the importance of these qualities?

Perhaps my background made me unable to relate to students at Northern. Not everyone was fortunate to have parents who revered education. I would try to make them see the value of learning—after all, knowledge is power—and not give up on them. Yet was it realistic for me, one individual, to change the minds of those teenagers who'd been raised without the drive to succeed at school? Parents like Michael's seemed to have been absent from their children's lives. I doubted I could make up for years of parental disinterest in a child's education. I was having enough trouble with students whose parents actually cared about their child's education.

That week passed with my students gradually assuming more control of the class, wearing me down with constant whining and disinterest. They were winning a battle I never wanted to fight. I wasn't sure how I could turn the tide. Daily, I was losing confidence I could make the classroom a place we would all enjoy.

That month's SOS class was cancelled, so I couldn't ask for the group's advice. Nabila was the only one left who could save me.

Amid the student lethargy before Thanksgiving break, Mrs. Dawkins arrived in my class, notebook in hand. I welcomed her with a relaxed smile. She sat in the back, long legs tucked neatly under a desk, as I presented a PowerPoint to my students about illnesses and remedies. Most students did not jot down the definition of new vocabulary words on worksheets I'd handed out.

Meghan and Amanda chatted; Michael put his head down to rest. Aravind doodled on his paper and Stephanie combed her hair and put on lip gloss.

I collected their notes on the PowerPoint—some papers were

blank so would get zeros—and I urged them to speak about what illnesses they regularly got. Some could ask what part of their body hurt and answer the question, but most struggled to form a sentence. Especially aware of Mrs. Dawkins' presence, I tried to show I cared, remaining energetic and enthusiastic throughout the lesson.

The bell rang, and students filed out. Mrs. Dawkins got up from her desk and approached me. She complimented me on my artistic ability in developing the presentation that drew her in with eye-catching photos and realistic sounds.

"But you know, you're working way too hard," she said. "It clearly took a lot of time to make the PowerPoint and then present it. You're doing too much, and the kids aren't doing enough. It should be just the opposite. You shouldn't feel exhausted after a lesson. They should."

*Everyone was giving me advice, and I was spending hours on lessons that fell flat. Nothing I did worked. What else could I do to be successful? I followed Nabila's advice but that too hadn't resulted in turning around the class. I was trying to get students to like me, but that proved very challenging.*

"How can I get them to work?" I asked.

She explained how my job wasn't to entertain kids, but to educate them, which meant they had to work hard every day. Before they left class, they had to show me they'd learned something new. Students didn't necessarily expect teachers to be creative or innovative, though it wouldn't hurt if I varied my routine. The same was true about incorporating technology into lessons. To develop focused lessons, she recommended I observe other teachers' classes.

"Why don't you go see a history class—or maybe an English one?" she said.

"I've already seen Nabila teach," I said, dejectedly.

*There it was again—the same advice. For some reason, I had no idea how to mimic in my class Nabila's style and competency. It was like magic how she controlled her students.*

"It'd be good for you to see other teaching styles," she answered. "You'll pick up ideas on how you can develop your own style—and how to incorporate informal assessments into every lesson."

*Every day I was including informal assessments, but students weren't taking them seriously. Couldn't Mrs. Dawkins tell my students to start working and respecting me?* It didn't seem fair my students didn't hold themselves to the high standards I hold them and myself to.

"Sure, I'll observe several classes," I said. "I hope it helps."

On a clear crisp morning after December's first snow dusting, I witnessed how Mr. Andrews made the Industrial Revolution come to life for fifteen spellbound freshmen in history class. In a round table discussion, students read passages about children working fifteen-hour days, locked inside grimy factories, as depicted in Charles Dickens's books. The students then discussed laws subsequently enacted to protect children and answered questions from a packet on the Industrial Revolution. Classroom behavior was calm and peaceful, just as I remembered it in my childhood. Mr. Andrews urged students to think about how they would react having to spend days at a workhouse instead of having the luxury of attending school. Several raised their hands to answer, giving responses that showed they'd absorbed key points about Dickens's England.

Mr. Andrews hadn't used a PowerPoint, video, or music—and yet, students were enthralled. The reason: He made the information relevant to their lives and inspired them to think. He expected them to think—and verbalize their impressions of a period they had known little about before. A semicircle made the activity more private and intimate—and helped keep students involved. I needed to utilize this effective teaching technique with my Dirty Dozen.

On a dreary winter day, I visited Dr. Donatello's honors English class. She admitted she was bored with teaching, but she hadn't found another job that paid as well, so decided to stay. Nevertheless, she exuded excitement as she taught a lesson on metaphors in "The Seafarer" by Ezra Pound. Students listened politely, no one misbehaved as she explained how Mr. Pound felt isolated as an expatriate, just like the seafarer moving from place to place. Did anyone in the room also feel distant from school, family, or friends, alienated from their surroundings as if they didn't belong? I almost raised my hand. No one readily opened up, but a few eyes quietly glistened. Dr. Donatello had successfully connected Mr. Pound's situation to her twenty-first century teenagers.

Dr. Donatello and Mr. Andrews both touched the hearts of their students by making their lessons relevant. Couldn't I do that as well? I wondered whether my students would welcome a new Madame Nelson, one who was trying harder to be a good teacher, even if unclear about the correct path to follow.

Over the next few days, I incorporated ideas from Dr. Donatello's and Mr. Andrews's lessons into my classes. Drawing from Dr. Donatello's lesson, I wrote on the board relevant questions about our unit: Do French teens wear similar clothes as Americans and where do they shop for clothes? Students now sat in desks arranged in a circle.

But none of these new techniques seemed to work. Students still refused to work. They told me I hadn't given them enough time to learn the vocabulary, grammar, and culture of clothes before expecting them to discuss the topic. I hadn't yet developed an essential question that excited them. Nabila recommended I develop a scenario: They had flown to Paris, but their suitcase didn't make it. They all needed new clothes. Where would they buy them and how much would they cost in Euros? What size were they in France? Everyone would make a PowerPoint to present to the class. The goal: I wouldn't try so hard; they would work more. What a great plan. With any luck, I'd soon be qualified to author *The Dummies Guide to Successful Classroom Teaching*.

A few days before the holiday break I gave a few colleagues, including Mrs. Dawkins, a snowman ornament and a card thanking them for their friendship and support. At the last minute, I included Leslie, hoping this would help change her opinion of me. But as I put the gift in her mailbox, I wondered if Frosty would be the only future reminder of my presence in these teachers' lives. Would I be gone for good by summer? I pictured Leslie during subsequent holidays, dangling Frosty from a branch on her Christmas tree, reading my name and date on the back, and remembering me. Would she regret letting me go? More likely, I feared, she'd be relieved. I was gone, no longer her problem.

# Fewer Students Major in Education

In 1970-71, 36% of all bachelor's degrees awarded to women were in education.

In 2018-19, 6% of all bachelor's degrees awarded to women were in education.

In the early 1970s, about 200,000 undergraduate degrees in education were awarded annually. In 2018-19, it was less than 90,000.

One reason for declining participation in undergraduate education programs is expanded opportunities available to women in other fields.

*Source: American Association of Colleges for Teacher Education. Colleges of Education: A National Portrait (2022).*

## Teacher Preparation Programs

In 2018-19, about 500,000 students enrolled in 1,700 teacher preparation programs.

Some 77% attended traditional programs at colleges and universities, while 11% attended 487 alternative programs.

Community colleges serve as the point of entry to higher education for almost 40% of students who eventually major in education at four-year institutions.

Despite efforts to recruit diverse students, colleges of education are not as racially and ethnically diverse as public schools where students will work.

In 2022, 55% of students in public schools are projected to be non-white, but only 28% of those earning undergraduate degrees and certificates from colleges of education are people of color.

*Source: American Association of Colleges for Teacher Education. Colleges of Education: A National Portrait (2022).*

## Chapter Thirteen

# SEÑORA CASEY

It was February 8th, the day of my second observation with Leslie. I plodded along a hallway toward my classroom, apprehensive about spending fifty minutes under my critical supervisor's scrutiny. Leaf-less windblown bushes scraped against the dark hallway windows as if to warn me about a foreboding day. Was there a hidden door where I could leave unnoticed? I could escape through a side door, skipping class, but then I'd automatically be fired. No, I needed a paycheck—and I still believed I could learn how to successfully teach these kids.

I entered the empty orderly classroom, the blackboard erased, the chairs in a neat semicircle. Within minutes, would students again wrestle the upper hand from me? Would they move chairs to be closer to each other, write their names on the board, and work on homework from other subjects? On this day, I couldn't afford to let them misbehave. Nabila had given me a game plan: Students would create a presentation about going on vacation on their laptops, using the past tense. They loved working on computers, so I was hopeful they wouldn't act up, and Leslie would find me competent. My stomach cramped up, as if it had been repeatedly punched. I pictured Leslie gloating over my failed lesson, her mission to oust me closer to completion. But perhaps my fears were unfounded—and all would go well.

As usual, I stood in the doorway greeting students. Not one student smiled or said "bonjour." I asked students to take a laptop from the cart and log in. A din of voices—in English—bombarded me: "What's my password?" "My computer is dead!" and "Where's the assignment?" I answered in French, but students looked at me as if I were crazy to try resolving technical issues in an unfamiliar language. I helped them individually in English, fearing from that second on, Leslie would view me as incompetent. "Important instructions were always to be given in the target language," I remembered her saying.

Once each student got a laptop, the class settled down. Students searched for pictures of vacation places, captioning them with sentences in the past tense about an imaginary trip. I circulated the room, helping them construct grammatically correct sentences and scolding them when I caught them using Google Translate. They hadn't yet mastered the past tense despite working on it for a week, so I decided to reteach it. On the board, I penned the conjugations of the verb *avoir* and its common past participles. Not surprisingly, no one looked up from their computer. Why should they? Google Translate had become their inappropriate go-to tool in French class. To impress Leslie, I had prepared a rubric for the project and printed out the assignment for students who couldn't find it online.

Much of the period, my students worked and enjoyed the hands-on activity. I glowed, feeling useful as I helped them. No one complained, napped, or talked back to me. It was one of our best days in class.

As the kids filed out of the classroom, I beamed. The lesson hadn't been a failure—two students even thanked me for it. Certainly, Leslie would see its qualities—and my improvement—and give me a passing grade.

Two weeks later at the post-observation conference, Leslie complimented me on a much better lesson than the one in the fall, noting my improvement in getting students to work. But then she bombarded me with criticism. In class, students still were shouting out in English, arriving late, and talking. My rapport with students was still strained and angry, my classroom management techniques non-existent, my lessons not engaging or relevant enough. She commended me on using technology, but I should have told students they would receive a zero if they used Google Translate. She scolded me for not having taught the past tense well enough before assigning the project.

"But we spent four days on it last week," I said, sitting in her sunny office near the library that windy February day. "They had worksheets, a listening exercise, and a speaking one. They should have mastered it. They just didn't work hard enough."

Leslie tilted back in her administrator's throne glaring at me with hawk-like piercing eyes. "It's your job to make them interested in French. Maybe your activities weren't engaging enough.

This is a student-centric district that values the whole child, and it seems that you're not considering their social-emotional health enough by establishing a positive rapport with them."

Wow, what about *my* social-emotional health? Was she portraying me as an uncaring, inconsiderate person who just threw random assignments at students without planning or thought?

"I've been trying my best to connect with students," I said. "At my previous teaching position in a Catholic school, the girls appreciated my teaching style and worked. They learned French."

Leslie's eyes flashed angrily. "You've got to forget what worked at the Catholic school. Public schools are completely different from parochial ones, and the sooner you realize that the better off you'll be."

She was right. I had to stop comparing Sacred Heart students with those at Northern.

"I didn't think the lesson was that bad," I said. "They were on task and working."

For a moment, Leslie softened. "I'll give you that. Also, you speak French well enough to teach high school."

A glimmer of hope entered the stifling office. "Nabila has been helping me with ideas on how to engage students. I've also observed several classes to learn about classroom management. I feel I'm improving."

Leslie was silent for a few seconds. She hadn't yet given up on me. "Look, you need to improve your rapport with students. The students still do not respect you. They don't see you as an authority figure—and until that happens, they won't learn. Why don't you observe one of Señora Casey's Spanish classes? You know her, right?"

What the heck! Another class to observe! I'd sat in several classes that I'd begun to joke with Nabila I'd regressed into a student teacher, a youngster fresh out of college, instead of a forty-something mother of three with five years teaching experience. Did Señora Casey possess a magic potion or innovative pedagogical tricks to make students respect me? Or would this be more of what I'd seen in other teachers' classes?

"Yes, we share a classroom at the middle school," I said. "We pass each other in the hall after morning classes."

"So you'd be open to sitting in on one of her classes?"

"Sure," I said grimly.

I couldn't refuse my supervisor. She was the one who could fire me. "Good. Keep meeting with Nabila. She's great with kids."

For a moment, Señora Casey's classroom felt like paradise. Several dozen students bustled about the spacious, modern room. Many mingled with friends, smiling and chatting amicably as if they hadn't seen each other for months, while others quietly sat down in the back of the room with their notebooks open. Sunlight from huge windows bathed metal desks in rows facing the chalk board.

The bell rang. Ignoring the start of the class period, students continued to socialize. This definitely wasn't heaven. It began to look like my class.

"Hey, you guys, stop making my life miserable and get in your seats," bellowed Señora Casey, in front of the classroom. "I don't have all day to wait for you. You messed up big time on your test."

Complaints ensued. "That test was unfair." "That test was freaking tough." "What the f*ck is conjugating verbs?" "Do you mean we have to memorize stuff?" They sounded like my obnoxious high school students—angry at a teacher and blaming her for their mediocre performance.

Señora Casey marched around the room, finally stationing herself in a cluster of girls who were wearing heavy makeup. She planted her iron-like legs on the floor, looking like a warrior ready for battle. Her face reddened slightly. Was she ready to ring their necks?

"Wait a minute. You've had two weeks to learn the verbs 'to have' and 'to be,'" she said. "You've done a lot of exercises on them—we even played a game. For the past month, we've gone over subject pronouns. Remember all the worksheets you guys did? What's the matter with you? You don't study enough. You waste time in class goofing off. You don't work. I'm not talking about the ones who got an A or B on the test—and many of you did. You guys did what you were supposed to do. You worked hard. You took the class seriously. More of you need to do that. You've got to get off your butts and start working. Do you expect to learn anything by just sitting there looking pretty? I don't think so."

Students' bodies froze, looking wide-eyed at Señora Casey.

"This time, I'm going to be kind and give you a second chance," she continued. "You can retake the test tomorrow. I'll take the average of both tests."

A few cried out claiming injustice. "What happens if I do worse on the second test?" "Why can't you just drop the lower grade?" "That's BS." "This is totally unfair."

*My God, they were worse than my students—and Leslie thought I could learn something from this chaotic gathering of misfits.*

"Watch your language," said Señora Casey. "Life is unfair. Deal with it. That's what it's like in the real world. Come here after school tomorrow if you want to take the new test."

Her words did not placate them. Señora got blasted with complaints about how they hadn't had enough time to study, the worksheets were too demanding, and grammar was super boring. Casey remained calm as if her outrage was part of her normal routine.

"Quit making excuses," she said. "Study. Get your work done. Learn Spanish. You can't be lazy and expect to get good grades. This is school."

I squirmed in my seat, appalled at her pejorative remarks. Could teachers really address their students so directly and honestly? To me, she was rude, but maybe that was how Leslie wanted me to be with my students. Yet Señora Casey had shown a caring attitude by allowing students to retake the test. Was it her tenure that protected her from administrator criticism?

I wondered if I could copy Señora Casey's caustic or irreverent or confrontational style. It wasn't my style. In public, I wanted to project an even-tempered woman with the prowess to get things done without resorting to anger. If I became as belligerent as Señora Casey, wouldn't students resent me even more? Nabila was a better model for me. Though I hadn't yet transformed into her, I'd been working on it, hopeful I could get there before year's end.

## Characteristics of a Bad Teacher

Teaching without empathy.

Failing to establish a lesson's relevance.

Making students feel dumb.

Arriving late and unprepared to class.

Personalizing students' responses.

Assuming a lesson taught is a lesson learned.

Assessing infrequently.

Calling only on volunteers to participate.

Ignoring discipline problems.

Getting easily intimidated.

## Chapter Fourteen

# PARENT MEETING

The following week in early March, Leslie asked me to attend a meeting in her office with Meghan and her mother. Several students had complained about my teaching—and Meghan was upset about her French grade. We needed to zero in on the problem and develop solutions.

As I walked to Leslie's office, I dreaded this meant she thought something was seriously wrong in my classroom. I expected to be blamed for any problems brought to Leslie's attention, including creating a toxic environment in which almost no learning took place.

In the long corridor, I glanced at the posters advertising past football and soccer games, breathing in the sanitized smell of recently cleaned floors. Everything was in order.

Leslie stood guard near her door with a stern face. I approached her, nervous she would once again lecture me about my failures. She reached out her hand to shake mine.

"I'm glad you could make it," she said with an accepting smile.

Her politeness and civility surprised me, a sliver of hope surfacing that this meeting might not culminate in my dismissal. "Meghan is a nice girl, but she could work harder," I said.

Leslie nodded. "Kids can be lazy. By the way, how did Señora Casey's class go?"

I hesitated. *How could I honestly tell her that I now even more seriously questioned if I belonged at Northern after witnessing contentious classroom management strategies?*

"She keeps students in line," I admitted. "But I have a very different personality. I don't know if her techniques would work for me."

*I was proud of my diplomatic response—and keeping silent about what I viewed as Señora Casey's semi-abusive behavior. To make it at this school, I would have to toughen up, but I wondered if I had what it takes to change that much. I'd been raised in an upper middle-class home, attending schools where authority was respected. That was my norm.*

"Señora Casey gets kids prepared for Spanish 2—that's all I ask for," said Leslie, escorting me into her office, closing the door behind her.

I sat down, kitty cornered to her desk, two empty chairs next to mine awaited. "She lets students retake quizzes. That seems fair."

"We don't want kids to fail here," she said smiling. "Look, about this meeting . . . Don't defend yourself in front of Meghan and Mrs. Baxter. Say that you understand their concerns and speak about strategies to help ease tensions between you and Meghan."

*Yes, I could do that, but I was fed up trying to adopt strategies from other teachers that were not a good fit for me. Perhaps I just didn't fit in. Maybe I should plan for a future outside education.*

"Okay," I said, my shoulders tensing up.

"Be sure to tell Meghan and her mom about your expectations and talk about your grading policy."

*I had to avoid confrontation: Just explain classroom procedures and expectations. Be logical, not emotional. Don't admit how I believed that my background was too different from students here to be able to relate to them. Don't argue with Leslie or Mrs. Baxter. Draw on all my upbringing as a diplomat's daughter to make the meeting amicable. How proud Dad and Mom would be that I had learned to get along with all sorts of people. They had raised me to avoid confrontation, advocating emphasizing similarities of opinions, while ignoring differences. By living in African and European nations much of my childhood, I had figured out how to adapt to different cultures. Certainly, this translated into knowing how to survive in this school's culture.*

"I'm not looking forward to this," I whispered.

"Other teachers have these meetings—and they do fine," she said. "Let's make it a productive one. It can't become a shooting match between you and Meghan—or even worse, her mom."

"That won't happen," I promised, as we heard a knock on the door.

Leslie got up to answer the door, and we both greeted the Baxters. Meghan's eyes averted mine; she looked like a Barbie doll with her slight build, bouncy blond hair, and perfect makeup. Her mom frowned, refusing to shake my hand.

"I understand that Meghan has some concerns about French class," Leslie said. "Mrs. Nelson is here to address your issues."

I had planned to start the meeting complimenting Meghan on her strengths—her intelligence and desire to succeed—then mention her weaknesses—disrespect, laziness, and poor attitude. But Mrs. Baxter took the lead.

"I'd like to start by saying what Meghan is telling me about French class," said Mrs. Baxter, a petite woman with piercing green eyes. "She tells me it's a joke with no one listening to the teacher. Her grade has gone down, and she says this is because Mrs. Nelson doesn't teach lessons. She comes home and says she has no idea what will be on a test."

*What about all the grammar and vocabulary I'd taught using*

*PowerPoints, Jeopardy games, and dialogues? She has no idea how many hours I spent creating activities that I'd prayed would work.*

Leslie cleared her throat, the commander-in-chief taking charge. "I've talked to Mrs. Nelson about classroom management, and she's working on that."

Mrs. Baxter's tiger-like eyes stared at me, her long fingernails gripping the arm rest pointing toward me.

*What should I say? Tell her how anxious I felt every day in her daughter's class and how my confidence was eroding as I failed even with help from colleagues? I wasn't even sure I cared if I got fired; the classroom was taking a toll on my well-being. Didn't Mrs. Baxter and her sassy daughter ever argue at home, and how did she handle those difficulties? Couldn't we band together to make Meghan realize that education is a two-way street, that if she wanted to succeed in class it wouldn't hurt to treat me with respect? That wasn't on the agenda. She felt to me like an adversary; could I turn her into a friend?*

"I tell students to listen to me when I teach," I said. "I've prepared engaging activities for them, such as PowerPoints and Jeopardy games, and it's up to them to work. They must be quiet to learn the language."

Leslie lowered her eyes, as if ashamed of me. But shouldn't students be quiet and respectful in class? Later I realized I should have said I wanted Meghan to succeed in French—and I'd help her do that.

"The district insists that students adhere to a strict code of conduct and behavior," said Leslie, her elbows resting on the oak desk. "Mrs. Nelson is aware of the consequences of students misbehaving in class."

I felt trapped, under attack, the oxygen in the room depleted. I glanced out the open window behind Leslie, wishing I could transform into a butterfly and fly outside.

I wanted to explain how I called parents many times, telling them their child had acted up, argued with me, refused to work, or talked out of line. I needed their support, but after a second call home, parents started to see *me* as the problem. I'd begun to lose confidence—and hope that I'd ever be able to change my class.

"Madame Nelson is unfair in how she grades," said Meghan, twirling her hair with her fingers. "Her tests are impossible. She expects us to know the material the next day. That's not going to happen."

*Some weeks I set high expectations for my students, but was that intensity wrong? Other weeks, after listening to their concerns, I modified lessons, giving them more time to master material. I was trying to not compare them to Sacred Heart students, who had memorized fifteen new vocabulary words each day with a quiz every ten days. This was making it even clearer to me that kind of rigor was impossible here.*

"We do believe that students should learn something new every day," piped in Leslie. "She has a curriculum to follow, which she's doing."

*Finally, support from Leslie.*

"Meghan, we always have a review before a quiz or test," I said defensively. "Don't you remember the Jeopardy game on daily routine?"

"I didn't understand the questions on that game," she said.

*Well, I almost explained, my students had arrived unprepared for French 2 after my predecessor had focused more on her sex life than teaching French. I wasn't to blame for that. No wonder she'd been fired, which could also be my destiny. Would that be so bad?*

"Before the review, just go over your notes—and bring them to class so you can use them for the game, okay?" I said.

Meghan looked annoyed, as though she was unused to being challenged.

"Yes, honey, take Mrs. Nelson's advice," said Mrs. Baxter, as she patted her daughter's shoulder. "Study a little each day. Don't cram."

*Wow, Mrs. Baxter backed me up. She was no longer the enemy. How good it felt to be appreciated—and from a parent who arrived at our meeting sided with her daughter. Could I ask her to encourage Meghan to be kinder by refusing to join students ganging up on me? Meghan was a leader. She could persuade classmates to show more respect to me. She could tell them to quiet down and listen to me because she wanted to learn French and get good grades. Together she and I could change the class's dynamics. But that meant Meghan would have to collaborate with a teacher, which took courage as she set aside loyalties to peers. That wouldn't happen unless she liked me.*

"It seems we've come to an understanding," said Leslie, glancing at all of us. "This has been a positive meeting for all parties."

Then, she summarized our discussion and recommended Meghan meet me for extra help during lunch or after school, encouraging her to finish assignments. I shook Mrs. Baxter's hand, wishing I could confide that Meghan was a sweet girl who unfortunately banded with troublemakers who seem intent on disrupting the class.

"That wasn't that bad," said Leslie, as she brushed aside papers. "But you've got to take charge of those kids. You can't let them run the show."

"You'll observe me once more, right?" I asked.

"Yes, sometime in late March or early April," she said.

It wasn't inevitable I'd be fired. The meeting hadn't been a shouting match. I still had a few months to transform into an acceptable teacher. Was I up for that challenge? I'd already fended off so many challenges. Did I care if my contract wasn't renewed the following year? I was getting tired of dreading work every single day.

## Communicating with Parents

Call or email when a child does something positive.

When a student is failing, contact a parent, well before the marking period ends. This gives the student time to rectify the situation.

Key message from teachers: "I want us to work together. You are your child's most important teacher."

What to Do at a Parent Meeting

Listen and ask questions.

Speak in a respectful and considerate way.

Address concerns with a problem-solving approach.

Keep a positive attitude about working together.

Mention a student's positive experiences.

Show respect for a student's background and cultural identity.

Recognize parent's emotional investment in their children.

Ask for parent's input to solve problems.

Remind the parent you, too, want their child to succeed.

## Chapter Fifteen

# LAST OBSERVATION

The day before my final observation, through the cafeteria windows, I eyed nature's transformation: trees blossomed into a palette of pastel colors resembling an Impressionist painting. A clear blue sky shone in the background. Spring was the season of renewal. Perhaps during that evaluation Leslie would see a new me, one who would impress her enough to keep me the following year. But like a delicate bud challenged by gusty storms, I felt fragile in my ability to withstand the kids' tempestuous personalities.

Nabila and I sat together at a round metal table eating lunch. She praised me for preparing a great lesson on parts of the body with a song, dialogue, and game. Leslie would be blown away, she said, and my contract renewed.

"Relax and have fun," she said, gobbling down a sandwich. "You'll be fantastic. Just follow the lesson."

"Thanks for believing in me," I said softly. "But I don't know if it's going to work. The kids still misbehave. Besides, Leslie doesn't want me here next year."

"Don't say that Jen," she said. "She'll see you've improved. You know, she loves songs in the classroom."

"What happens if my students hate the song?" I said, chewing on carrot sticks.

"Most kids adore songs," she said, zipping up her lunch bag. "Sing along with them. Don't use one with complicated lyrics. That will confuse them."

"Okay. But I don't think they'll like it."

"Jen, be positive. It will work. We've gone over the lesson."

"They're going to take charge—like they always do," I said. "I'm like a mouse to them—and they're cats. I'm scared of them. They can claw me unless I hide."

Nabila laughed. "Show them your funny side, okay? Kids learn when they're having fun."

I kept picturing Leslie as an alpha cat, blocking my escape route, as she bit into me, while my students gleefully watched me being devoured.

When I entered the classroom, I spotted a looming figure in the back, a big grin on her face like a Cheshire cat. It was Leslie. My breathing quickened as I tried to psych myself into believing I could impress her in a last-ditch effort to save my job. I'd be confident, in control, and powerful, pretending this was another normal day with my French 2 students. I banished thoughts of surrendering to them—and inhaled deeply to calm my nerves, knowing full well my fate would be sealed that afternoon.

For months I'd developed a backup plan just in case I was dismissed that involved applying for jobs outside education, perhaps even returning to journalism, or focusing on dating again with the goal of finding a rich guy who wouldn't expect me to earn a living. But I thought of myself as a working woman and liked the independence that came with making money.

Stationing myself near the blackboard, I started with a dialogue about visiting the doctor. Initially no one volunteered to play roles, though Stephanie and Elizabeth were finally persuaded after I promised them extra credit points. As usual, half the class forgot pencils, so I distributed a writing instrument. Michael blurted out that the lesson was boring, and Meghan announced that two girls in the lunchroom had found a cockroach. Some worked to answer the dialogue's questions, others looked lost. It was a typical period for us.

I prayed that singing the French version of "Heads, Shoulders, Knees, and Toes" would turn around the lesson. If we belted out the lyrics of the song, our voices harmoniously blending, we'd finally connect to each other. The past months' misery would melt away.

I sang along to the YouTube video projected on the board, urging students to join me. They refused, looking at me with disgust as if I had required them to eat escargots. I finished singing the entire song alone, my face red with embarrassment.

In the back of the classroom Leslie smiled diabolically, seemingly taking pleasure in my humiliation.

"Why didn't you all join in?" I asked the class.

"I don't like to sing in class," said Aravind, openly.

Others nodded in agreement, then admitted their insecurities: "I don't sing in public," said Michael honestly. "The song is too fast. I can't follow it," added Meghan, her eyes showing some regret. "It's not cool to sing," said Amanda. "That song sounded like it was for babies."

I couldn't win with this crowd, though frankly it was the reaction I had expected. My high schoolers didn't like singing, though in Nabila's classes they were open to it. Granted, they'd have preferred hip songs by Carla Bruni and Yannick, but they wouldn't have understood the lyrics.

I asked them if they'd filled in the lyrics on the worksheet. Again, cries of "How do you spell these words?" "Man, this is way too hard," and "We've never done this before. How do you do it?"

I cringed. Leslie texted on her cell phone. Yet I didn't give up, helping them with the necessary words.

Then, to perk up the class, I announced that we would play Simon Says using vocabulary of body parts and commands. I explained the rules in English. Leslie would disapprove, but students would be less confused. The game began.

A few students lethargically rose from their seats, but the majority balked at moving an inch. What should I do? Grab their armpits and raise them up as if they were puppets? So much for trying to incorporate the kinesthetic learning style when students preferred to chill.

Luckily I anticipated this and executed Plan B, where students remained seated for the game. They raised their legs under their desks, lifted their arms, and closed their eyes. Some students participated; others zoned out. Leslie gazed at her cell phone.

The lesson ended with my collecting the dialogue's comprehension questions, the all-important informal assessment. Several couldn't find their paper, complaining that this assignment should not be worth points. I answered it was, and they argued this was unfair. I ignored their whining. It was a normal lesson—not extraordinary or horrible—but certainly not good enough to pass the final evaluation, I feared.

I felt like a flop and suspected I wouldn't be rehired. A wave of sadness descended upon me as I reflected on how hard I'd worked that year, listening to teachers' advice and planning creative lessons, but to little avail. I had tried to like students, but I still saw them as tough and mean. I hadn't developed the expertise—and maybe the heart—necessary to work with these teenagers.

Despite Northern's decent salary and structure, did I want a second year at the school if it meant a repeat of the abuse I experienced during the first? It depressed me to think about leading a class again, as I hadn't yet figured out how to have fun teaching. I just needed to survive until June 18. What activities would make the next ten weeks bearable?

The following days, as the warmth of late spring crept through the windows, my classroom completely transformed into a minefield of conflicts exploding at any time. Occasionally I'd call in sick, after a restless night filled with nightmares in which students ousted me, assuming power, and I was too exhausted to fight back. I worried about getting the dreaded letter in my mailbox saying I was fired. Yet I continued my fruitless attempts to develop a rapport with students, allowing them to retake quizzes and offering them cookies after completing an assignment. Oddly enough, the cookies motivated only two students to finish the work, with others shouting out they didn't like Chips Ahoy. What the heck! If Chips Ahoy, the quintessential American sweet, didn't entice them to work, what would—chocolate cake with fudge frosting, pizza with pepperoni and sausages? Bringing them goodies was my Hail Mary pass, and even that failed. What was wrong with these kids? The monthly SOS meetings—for first-year teachers—provided no concrete solutions for disciplining unmotivated, low-achieving students. Besides, it was too late in the school year for miracles to happen.

Every day I anxiously checked my mailbox in the middle school for an official letter requesting a meeting, encouraging me to bring a union representative. This began the process of firing an employee. Leslie's evaluation was scathing, a clear indication that the district no longer believed in me. Honestly, I didn't belong at this high school, so maybe it would be a blessing to leave. But I still felt dejected, a dull pain lingering inside me, my confidence eroded about my capabilities as an educator. It hurt to be rejected, my sense of security dulled and future blurry.

Just before spring break, I received the much-anticipated letter on district letterhead in my mailbox. "We would like to meet with you to discuss your future employment at Northern High School. Please be advised that you may bring a union representative to this meeting," said the letter. I reread the words, stifling a wave of despair and smothering an impulse to sob. My lips quivered as I processed the news, alone with my thoughts in a mail room, with dozens of rectangular, wooden cubbies, though only mine had harbored a life-changing letter. How I wanted Nabila to console me, hug me, tell me I'd be okay, but she taught first period. Instead I rushed to the union rep's science classroom, hoping it was his prep period; he'd help me figure this out.

Marty's classroom was empty, so he had to be in the science lab concocting magical potions; perhaps one of them could help me. I gingerly knocked on the door, nervous about how to divulge my failure to anyone but Nabila. Marty in a white lab coat answered, and I hesitantly explained the situation, asking him if I should fight the dismissal, since I had made progress this year, but required a second one to become competent?

"No, that would make matters worse," said Marty, a beaker in his hand. "It's best you resign and look for another job in September. I've known teachers who were let go and went on to become

Teacher of the Year. Don't take it personally. Leslie fires lots of teachers. She's hard to get along with."

His words soothed me, though I wasn't sure I'd ever teach again. Marty admitted how he was considering leaving education—he was tired of the same routine and the kids wearing him down—and preferred working full time with the union. He'd be moving on in the next year or two. Evidently, others were not as happy here as I thought.

In the faculty room during lunch, I broke the news to Nabila.

"Maybe you were confused about which teacher to follow," she said. "You know how too many cooks spoil the broth?"

Certainly my year would have been easier if I'd read a manual with one set of procedures to follow. But teaching isn't scientific; it is an art that demands energy, creativity, and commitment. "I worked so hard this year," I pleaded. "And look where it got me!"

Nabila hugged me as I fought back tears. Failure felt embarrassing, but humbling. I had to learn from this failure, though this didn't mean I would always be a failure. I had kept trying until the last month when students had demoralized me, my strategies to control misbehavior lame and ineffective. I had shown little compassion toward students who failed a class because they didn't work. Those who busted their butts to learn the material but still hadn't passed—like me—deserved empathy.

"I've lost a few jobs before," I said. "But it was never because of poor job performance. This time it was."

"Don't think that way," she said. "Teaching is tough—and Leslie wasn't supportive of you. What you've got to do is look for another job right away. Take off a few days. Call in sick. Schools are now posting openings online. You'll have a better chance if you get in early."

But I never wanted to go through such an emotionally draining experience that left me defeated, questioning my abilities as a leader and professional. In a sense I was relieved to be saying goodbye to Northern, though I'd miss Nabila. This failure would not define me; I had learned from my mistakes and wouldn't repeat them.

I would reinvent myself. There was no reason for despair.

Nevertheless, I felt anxious the morning of my meeting with Leslie and Vice Principal Murphy. I wanted to skip it, but Marty reassured me that administrators would be kind, aiming to make it as painless—and pleasant—as possible for everyone. They didn't delight in being the messenger of bad news.

Leslie and Vice Principal Murphy were quietly conversing, sitting opposite each other, when Marty and I entered the orderly office. Marty patted me on the back, whispering that I should let him do the talking. I could voice my concerns, but I shouldn't argue with their findings nor refuse to resign. The district had deemed me unfit, lacking in essential qualities needed to work with teenagers; it was too late to change this decision. I promised I wouldn't cry; I'd already done plenty of that over the previous nine months. I wanted it over—five minutes tops to suffer through another humiliation.

Surprisingly, the meeting went better than expected. Marty spoke the most, though I asked if it would be possible to work part-time at the middle school where I believed I'd been successful. Leslie shook her head; they needed someone to teach both levels, and though left unsaid, I had the impression she hadn't been that pleased with my performance there.

Vice Principal Murphy lightened the mood by chatting about his summer plans and asking us about ours. Everyone but me mentioned travelling to visit family and friends, taking day trips to the shore, and starting home improvement projects. I didn't talk about my upcoming trip to France with my three teenagers, too engrossed in sadness about my dismissal. I wasn't in the mood for gaiety or small talk, but I never shed a tear. I was relieved they hadn't highlighted my faults to justify firing me; instead, they said the job hadn't been a right fit for me. But in a sense, I was qualified for the job; I spoke French fluently and came with three years' teaching experience at a Catholic school. It just was the kids: We hadn't liked or appreciated each other enough.

In mid-May, at a lunchtime tutoring session for the final exam, Meghan confessed that her peers had been testing me all year. "Don't worry. Next year, we'll be better," she said. "You weren't that bad."

*Really? They put me through this hell as a test?*

"Merci, Meghan," I said. "Your French improved this year."

She seemed to have forgotten about the parent meeting in winter when I told her she should work harder.

"I liked how we did the PowerPoint in your class," said Meghan, smiling at me, her final exam study guide in front of her.

*That was one of the few good days in class. That lesson on daily routine had been a success; it was too bad we hadn't had more of them.*

"You know, other students in our class appreciate how you drilled us in good study habits," she added.

"Like what?" I said, thinking about how often students came into class with I-don't-give-a-shit-about-this-class-or-teacher attitude.

"Little things like always doing homework, studying every night, and coming prepared to class," she said. "I want to go to a good college, and those skills are going to be super important."

So I wasn't a complete failure. Finally, a compliment after all the complaints and criticisms. It was these moments that teachers strove for. I glowed, realizing I had made a difference in the life of at least one student.

After Memorial Day weekend, students had absolutely no interest in learning. In my class, students raved about conquering the waves at the Jersey shore, sleeping all day, and partying all night. Even the little bit of order I had previously been able to maintain washed away. Most days I felt like crying as the minutes ticked slowly. Just like my students, I was exuberant about the prospect of summer's freedom, but couldn't it come quicker? I envied a colleague on medical leave since early May. Couldn't I be diagnosed with depression or anxiety so I could get away from these kids? A week later, my wish was partially granted: Nabila took over my French 2 Period 7 class and I taught only at the middle school in the morning.

*Finally, a burden was lifted—and I looked forward to restful sleep, dreaming of a bright future with no students.*

"Leslie understands how tough it's been for you," said Nabila. "This is best for the students and you. You'll get paid, and the district will pay me a little something."

"But what about my students?" I asked. "Won't they say anything about getting a new teacher?"

"I wouldn't worry about that. They're kids. They'll think something happened to you, so they got a substitute. That's what happened with Natalia."

Natalia, a Spanish teacher in her first year at Northern, had taken off time after a bout with depression and had yet to return.

She'd been an excellent teacher—no classroom management issues and students learned Spanish. Leslie hadn't renewed her contract. She didn't like Natalia. She was another one of Leslie's casualties.

"I won't say goodbye to them," I said, reflectively. "They would cheer as I left."

"It's tough for new teachers. Kids mistreat them. You're not alone."

I pictured thousands of new teachers struggling for nine months, working harder than they ever had, and finally by June, bonding with kids or feeling like strangling them.

"Without you, this year would have unbearable," I said, wiping tears from my cheek.

She hugged me as I stifled an outpouring of emotion. "You'll be fine. You've got to email me when you get an interview. Lots of schools will be interested in you."

"You never give up on me, do you?" I said, my lips quivering. "Thanks for taking care of me."

For her, I'd try my best to succeed at my next job—wherever it might be.

"You're going to be great at some school," she said. "You care about kids. You speak French well, and you're fun. Just relax. Take what you've learned here and make it work for you."

"I hope you're right," I said, sniffling. "I'm going to France this summer with my kids. I'm not sure I can afford it. It's the wrong time to spend money on travel."

"You'll qualify for unemployment this summer," said Nabila. "And in the fall, you'll have a full-time teaching job. You'll have plenty of money."

"We'll have picnics with bread and cheese," I said. "Forget eating at fancy restaurants."

"It's a once-in-a-lifetime experience for your kids," said Nabila. "Besides, you'll get away from the stress here. You'll relax. Drink some wine. Take walks. You can bring authentic materials to use in the classroom next year. It will be good for you."

I was relieved that I'd already paid for the flight and apartment in Paris. I would put on hold buying another car— with any luck, my aging minivan would keep chugging along another year without costly repairs. In September, I'd put myself on a strict budget, and get a paying job no matter what. Child support and alimony payments were still coming in. The future wasn't that grim—and the idea of dating someone with means was still in the back of my mind.

"I talked to Vice Principal Bangler yesterday. He knows I'm leaving and wanted to wish me well. He asked me if I knew where I'd be in ten years—I told him I didn't think I'd be teaching."

Nabila looked at me squarely in the eyes. "Of course you'll be teaching. What else would you be doing? Return to writing for a newspaper?"

That's when I told her about my plans to write, perhaps enroll in an MFA program in creative writing, and take the Foreign Service exam to become a diplomat like my dad. We all knew Mr. Bangler didn't like his job, and other administrators weren't pleased with his performance. I wasn't alone in how I felt about Northern. What did the stars have in store for us?

"Jen, don't give up on teaching," said Nabila. "You've gotten so much better over the year. I don't want to see that go to waste."

★ ★ ★

It was my last day at Northern. That morning was reserved for faculty to tidy up classrooms, hand in keys, and say goodbye to colleagues; students had left the day before in a chaotic, jubilant exit of hugs, tears, and high fives about how they had survived the year. I said goodbye to my middle school students, wishing them a good summer and praising them for learning French.

I walked through the empty corridor near what used to be my French 2 classroom, the metal lockers open, devoid of textbooks, pencil cases, and notebooks. It was eerily quiet without students roughhousing, gossiping, and rushing to their next class. I breathed a sigh of relief, marveling at the school's peacefulness. How come I hadn't been able to calm down my students?

Their voices echoed in my head. Perhaps I hadn't listened to their concerns early enough in the school year. I could have re-taught the French 1 curriculum in September, then the outcome might have been different. But I shouldn't be so harsh on myself; I wasn't the only one to blame for this ending.

Potato chip bags and granola bar wrappers no longer littered the hallway as I made my way to the exit, the one my students used to board buses. Freedom for them—and now for me. Was I going home permanently to my own kids, a new future, a new me?

I pushed open the side door to the parking lot, a slight breeze caressing me. Whisking away a feeling of melancholy, I headed toward my old minivan. No more days of waking up with dread in my heart. I stepped in my car, turned the key in the ignition, and felt the car roll away toward an uncertain, but exhilarating future. I was determined never to go back to teaching.

## What Gets Teachers Fired

Immoral conduct

Incompetence

Neglect of duty

Substantial noncompliance with school laws

Conviction of a crime

Insubordination

Fraud or misrepresentation

*Source: findlaw.com*

## Chapter Sixteen

# CHANGING DIRECTION

*A*fter the disastrous year at Northern, I vowed never to teach
again. But how was I going to make a living in a job that
made me happy? Perhaps I could return to journalism, become a
diplomat, or write full-time. I could see myself studying again. It
was time to figure out the next chapter in my life, but first I
needed a break from it all.

In France I wouldn't dwell on my troubles, and if I did, my
longtime friend Peggy would help steer my thoughts to the adventure at hand—of enjoying a country we both loved.

How Peggy and I laughed after sampling Calvados, a brandy
made from apples, at a Normandy vineyard. We almost gagged on
the bitter, high proof cider, its acrid taste reminding me of my
Northern students. No way would either of us drink Calvados
again. But we bought a bottle, anyway, as a thank you after a
lengthy tour with the distillery's owner. Would we bring the bottle
back to the United States? Probably not.

I wrapped the bottle in a sweater, sticking it in a corner of my
suitcase. As we navigated country roads in a stick shift Renault, I
worried the bottle would crack, the burnt orange liquor leaking
onto my clothes. In a hotel in a Normandy village, I suggested
Calvados as an aperitif before going out for dinner. We could
empty the bottle during the trip if every night we drank a glass.

Peggy opted out, and I didn't want to drink alone. The unopened bottle stayed protected in my suitcase.

At restaurants, Peggy and I sampled tasty local red and white wines. Most days I didn't obsess about my unclear future. But occasionally, as we wandered around cobblestone villages or ate dinner at a two-star restaurant, I sought Peggy's advice. What did she think about my joining the Foreign Service or studying for a PhD in journalism at a university in California so I could teach at a university, while living near my aging mother? Should I commit to a writer's life and enroll in an MFA program in creative writing?

Peggy approved of many of these options. Key, she said, was finding work that paid well enough that I would never live in squalor—even as a retiree. She encouraged me to study for the Foreign Service exam; a career in the State Department was exciting and offered good salaries. Pursuing a doctorate in journalism sounded way too long and costly and would provide no compensation for years. Before studying for an MFA program, she encouraged me to find out what types of jobs were available to graduates. Lastly, she advised, I shouldn't give up on teaching at a public school.

She was confident I'd soon find a way to earn a living. Frankly, teaching was high on her list of possibilities for me. I argued that I couldn't go through the hell of working at a public school again. She guaranteed my feelings about the profession would change if I found the right school. Her mottos: Keep your options open. Reinvent yourself. Don't be afraid of change.

Throughout the trip I'd suggest ways to dispose of the Calvados bottle. I didn't want to throw it in the trash. What a waste of hard liquor! What about giving it to a person who enjoyed Calvados? Someone might even pay us for it. We joked about peddling it to a hotel clerk, waiter, or a random pedestrian in Paris. But did anyone want a bottle full of a liquid that tasted worse than medicine?

After a week my kids arrived, and Peggy flew home—leaving me with the Calvados. I briefly thought about offering sips of it to my children. I pictured their disgust as they swallowed a capful, spitting it out, and telling me it was nasty. Why would a mom do that to her kids? I'd justify it as an introduction to one of France's centuries-old culinary delights.

The night before our flight home, I debated whether I should pack the bottle of Calvados. On the plane it could break, and at home my family would not drink it. But it held special memories of my lighthearted days with Peggy. It strangely now become part of France's charm: centuries old vineyards managed by women tied to the land. I couldn't leave it behind in a Paris hotel room. For protection I wrapped it in socks, placing it in my suitcase surrounded by shorts, shirts, and sandals.

I was relieved it survived the trip across the ocean. Not one crack in its hard glass. I brought home a piece of French culture, reminding me of carefree times in France, even if the liquor tasted bitter. I stored the bottle in my antique alcohol cabinet, offering it to guests daring enough to sample a drink as strong as vodka. I also used it in French cooking, but the burnt-off alcohol left an unsavory taste in each dish. I realized later I'd lugged a bottle of unpalatable alcohol all over France, while simultaneously carrying the weight of last year's painful memories in French class. Would I ever savor the sweetness of the apples in Calvados or would the drink always remain distasteful?

★ ★ ★

After the trip, in late August, I took Peggy's advice and applied for a teaching job at several public schools. Not one job came through; I was relieved. I needed time to create a new future, perhaps as a diplomat or writer. To make ends meet, I'd substitute teach several days a week.

Life across the seas tempted me. As a diplomat, I imagined exploring new cities, learning about different cultures, and dating a sophisticated foreigner. By joining the Foreign Service, I'd follow in my father's footsteps; how proud he would be. I'd forsake my mundane East Coast existence, where I only drove a minivan, shopped, and taught. I could explore different nations. Maybe I could visit Timbuktu's mud-and-timber mosques; trek through the Himalayas; and see Victoria Falls. As a State Department public relations officer, I'd write press releases and talk to the media about American policy; in the evening I'd attend swanky cocktail parties with high-level officials. My life would again be an adventure, as it had been as a child when I'd lived in Morocco, Egypt, and England.

I ordered a book on preparing for the Foreign Service exam. Its advice: Read *Time* or *Newsweek* for years (or even decades), listen to *NPR* daily, and watch nightly the *PBS Newshour*. I panicked. I hadn't done all of that. The book provided practice tests, and several hundred pages on American history, economics, politics, and the arts. I decided I'd ace the test by mastering all the material.

That fall and winter, I sequestered myself in my home office, diligently taking notes on the book's contents, memorizing key facts and figures. As a diplomat, I would have to explain my country to foreigners; knowledge was key to my success. Very rarely did I think about how Northern students were faring under another teacher or if Leslie was having fun with her new victim French teacher.

One Saturday morning in February, after five months of studying, I drove to the testing location at a community college not far from Northern. Memories of my time there flooded back. I desperately needed to pass the written test—and the other two sections of the application process—so I would never again teach at a school like that. Certainly, the online multiple choice test with a timed writing section couldn't be that complicated. But it was challenging. I guessed on questions that made little sense to me, though the writing prompt didn't faze me, and I penned what I thought was a decent essay. No wonder 50 to 70 percent of test takers failed the test. I prayed I wouldn't be one of them.

Weeks later, I got the results in an email from the State Department. I had passed the test. Hallelujah! All the hours of studying had paid off; I was confident I could be on my way to becoming a diplomat. Now on to the second part of the process of writing five essays about how my life experiences had prepared me for a State Department career. I discussed growing up overseas, teaching in the Peace Corps and at public American high schools, and writing for newspapers and magazines. I felt positive that I would breeze through the second entry gate into the State Department. I needed to start preparing for the oral exams in Washington, DC. I reached out to my brother, who'd passed the written test, about his strategies for succeeding in the final step of the process. But the agency hadn't been impressed with my phase two replies; I wasn't invited to the oral exams. What the heck! Why didn't they view me a qualified candidate?

For several days I moped about the house, another failure weighing on me. After the initial shock subsided, I contemplated studying Arabic and reapplying the following year—the Foreign Service gave priority to candidates with knowledge of a "critical needs language"—and then I'd surely be accepted. But to master Arabic, I needed hundreds of hours of class time, and this even after having studied it for two years while attending high school in Egypt. There was no guarantee after passing all the test's components I'd be offered a job. Some years, few openings existed for new Foreign Service officers.

Besides, would my family have approved of moving abroad? My ex-husband would have hated me for taking our children away; they too might have objected to leaving home. I let go of my desire to change my life so dramatically.

So, what was plan B? Could I ever earn a living through writing the way I had done it as a reporter? It was a long shot returning to journalism after years out of the profession. Yet even without remuneration, I enjoyed creating stories that I shared with my writing group and at writing workshops. Was it time for me to begin thinking of myself as an author? I doubted I was literary enough to join those prestigious ranks, among those who might hold graduate degrees in creative writing. After researching MFA programs, I discovered that, with this terminal degree, I could teach writing at colleges and universities. I applied to several low-residency MFA programs. If accepted, I would attend classes on campus twice a year for ten days, the remaining time working from home. During the first residency, I'd determine if the program was worth the time and money. After all, as a journalist, hadn't I learned to write?

At Vermont College of Fine Arts, in my 40s, I found an artistic community of sympathetic, committed writers who didn't worry about making money. That first semester, I learned about significant differences between journalism and literature: for the first time, I could enjoy lingering with a piece, reflecting on its deeper meaning, using craft elements like metaphors and slanted details, and revising to make my prose sing. I could focus more on putting feeling into my stories and less on facts. I needed this education. I decided I'd dive whole-heartedly into the program—and seek a teaching job to pay tuition.

Back in New Jersey that summer, I aced an interview for a part-time, maternity leave position at Easton, a nearby prep school. The next school year, every morning, I taught three hour-long classes with twelve students per class. Students behaved—they didn't want to be kicked out of their pricy, prestigious school. I was happy that I was earning more than substitute teaching while being afforded afternoons off to work on my MFA.

Teaching at the school, around an oval-shaped table, I regained my faith in teenagers; they worked as hard as the Catholic girls and spoke French even better. Among the students was a girl from the wealthy, philanthropic Rockefeller family, and she wasn't pretentious or snobby.

I began to enjoy teaching again: No discipline problems, teens with attitudes, or nasty supervisors. I spoke only French in class—at a rapid clip—and students understood me. I relaxed, and my funny side finally emerged with kids laughing in class. By Thanksgiving break, I'd forgotten how much I had once dreaded teaching.

To earn extra cash, I tutored public school students in their homes. I loved it when a teenager came from my kids' nearby high school, since it meant I could easily drop by to discuss issues or pick up work from the regular teacher. I still questioned if I had what it took to succeed in a public school—and observing Mrs. Greenbaum, a first-year teacher there, reminded me of my previous struggles.

\* \* \*

That May, Mrs. Greenbaum, a middle-aged woman, looked exhausted as she greeted me, the sun casting shadows in an empty classroom, strewn with chewing gum wrappers and pencil stubs on the floor. She handed me two assignments for Courtney, an eleventh grader with an anxiety disorder whom I was tutoring. "I'm glad to hear that all's well with Courtney," she said. "She's such a nice girl."

Could she say the same thing about my daughter, Emily, who was also in her French 4 class? Emily had labeled Mrs. Greenbaum a pushover; over the winter, students had taken control of the classroom, transforming into mini-CEOs. Mrs. Greenbaum cried when kids didn't follow instructions, losing even more credibility with them. She misplaced handouts, lost quizzes, and put incorrect grades in the grade portal. If a student complained about a low grade, she'd automatically raise it as if she had made a mistake. If someone objected to a project's due date or complexity, she'd change it. French class had become a joke: everyone got an A and no one learned anything. Emily hated the class; Mrs. Greenbaum probably did too.

"Should I use this rubric to grade the professions project?" I asked, pointing to a handout.

She nodded. "Courtney won't need much help. She's a good student."

"She got an A- on the grammar test," I said, handing it to her. "She wanted to know if you have a study guide for the final exam."

"Not yet," she said. "She should start reviewing old packets."

"I can't believe it's almost the end of the year."

"It's been a tough year for me," said Mrs. Greenbaum. "The kids have been challenging."

*Was the teacher partially responsible for their misbehavior?*

"I hope Emily didn't give you a hard a time," I said, pulling up a desk next to hers. "She can be strong-willed and opinionated."

Mrs. Greenbaum sighed, nervously straightening up papers

on her desk. What could she say to a parent? She was too well-mannered to badmouth Emily.

"Yes, she makes it known what she thinks. Others are much worse."

That was good news. Should I suggest that Mrs. Greenbaum listen to Emily's advice about how to improve the class? While watching Emily babysit, I'd discovered her teaching skills: She was strict, firm, fair, and consistent, but also fun loving and playful. It seemed that Mrs. Greenbaum didn't like her students, and they had picked up on that.

"Sometimes, I don't get along with Emily," I said. "She's a tough cookie. Do you have summer plans?"

"I'll be looking for a job," she said. "I doubt I'll be rehired here."

She could be experiencing the end-of-the-year anxiety that comes from the uncertainty of a contract renewal. But maybe she already knew she didn't fit in there.

"It didn't work out for me at one school," I admitted, ashamed about my dismissal. "I didn't get along with the kids. But this year at Easton prep school, it's been good. I'm taking over for a woman on maternity leave. Maybe you could find a teaching position at a private school?"

She leaned back in her chair, distancing herself from me. "No, I think I'm done with teaching. Would you be interested in this job?"

*Should I consider working in the same district as my kids?*

"Emily wouldn't want me to work at her school," I said. "Besides, I want a part-time job. I'm working on a graduate degree in creative writing."

"That sounds interesting," she said, smiling. "A lot better than teaching."

She explained that as a divorcee with two kids, she needed

full-time work. She was leaning toward finding a job in business, so she could work with adults. She couldn't handle what she believed were unkind teenagers.

"Good luck finding another job," I said. "I'll be looking for a more permanent job too, and it could be in teaching."

It was too late to tell Mrs. Greenbaum that one of the secrets to successful teaching was liking students. She'd given up on that long ago. I remembered my children's comments about their teachers: the good ones, they loved; the bad ones, they hated; and the mediocre ones, they ignored. Students mocked and teased ineffective teachers but worshipped the good ones.

How Emily had raved about Mr. Johnson, her cute, twenty-something chemistry teacher whom she often revealed she'd marry—even though he was engaged. He made class fun, joking with students and caring about their progress. After school he tutored students, calmly explaining the intricacies of atoms, molecules, and ions. He could relate to less brilliant students—he too had struggled in school. He simplified the material and, at least for Emily, it worked. I could make French easy and simple, just like Mr. Johnson, though I doubted I had the same attraction as a young, newly minted teacher.

My two boys joked about Emily's crush on Mr. Johnson. How could she think he'd want to marry her? That was ridiculous. Teachers were off limits to students—everybody knew that—but it didn't stop teenage infatuation. Later, I had some experiences with teenage guys eyeing me suggestively.

For my son Patrick, Mrs. Brown was the best accounting teacher ever. She showed the same qualities as Mr. Johnson: caring, calm, consistent, and clear. No surprises or confusion in class, daily procedures enforced, and not-too-taxing work. Students didn't have to take notes or listen to boring lectures. Instead, they would focus on projects and work with friends; that way, they'd have fun and rave about the class.

My son Nicholas offered his advice on how I could become a better teacher. "Don't be Hitler!" he said. He hated authoritative, inflexible, and commanding educators, much preferring humorous ones who made learning fun.

My own children offered me solutions from the trenches of their high school experiences.

1. **Talking Students:** When completing an assignment, if students are talking across the classroom to each other and dis- rupting others, let them sit next to each other and chat. But if they don't finish the activity during class, they don't receive points. Never let them see your frustration or allow them to be the center of attention. Don't lose your cool!

2. **Sleeping Students**: Wake them up by dropping a book on their desk. A simple nudge—my normal procedure—isn't dramatic enough. The whole class finds it funny watching students who dare sleep in class get scared by the noise. Make sure to be the- atrical, so students understand that it's intended to be fun.

3. **Cheating Students**: That's easy: Follow procedures. Teachers should not make up the punishment. If a student cheats on a quiz or test, it's a zero. Everyone should know that. The teacher must be vigilant and catch students cheating using their cell phone or by putting answers on a paper shoved up their sleeve.

Armed with my kids' words of wisdom, I felt more confident I could succeed at a public school. But who knew when that would be? The following year, after several temporary teaching jobs, I felt even more prepared to join the ranks of successful teachers.

## Characteristics of Boarding Schools

Challenging academic environment

Community service requirement

Acceptance to highly selective universities

High tuition costs

Low student-teacher ratios

Nearly half of families receive financial aid

90,534 students attend 254 boarding schools

*Source: thebestschools.org and National Center for Education Statistics*

### Top Boarding Schools

**1.  Phillips Exeter Academy (Exeter, NH)**

Tuition, room, and board: $61,121
Number of students: 1,096
Unofficial feeder school for Harvard
Free tuition for families earning less than $75,000

**2.  Phillips Academy (Andover, MA)**

Tuition, room, and board: $66,290
Number of students: 1,130
Original feeder school for Yale
Oldest boarding school in the country

**3.  The Putney School (Putney, VT)**

Tuition, room, and board: $66,100
Number of students: 232
Acceptance to Yale, Dartmouth, Columbia
Students urged to pursue personal academic interests

**4.  Church Farm School (Exton, PA)**

Tuition, room, and board: $48,000
Number of students: 117
Acceptance to Carnegie Mellon, Cornell, MIT
Episcopal heritage

### 5. Episcopal High School (Alexandria, VA)

Tuition, room, and board: $66,360
Number of students: 440
Acceptance to William and Mary, Duke, Wake Forest
Signature Washington Program

*Source: 2021 study from thebestschools.org and schools' websites*

# Chapter Seventeen

## CLASSROOM CLASHES

"**F**uck off," said Anne, a sixteen-year-old student. "I don't want to see that face of yours near me."

I froze. Never had a student thrown that word at me before. I didn't expect this at Harris High School, a suburban school built in the 1960s.

It was my third week of teaching—I had started after Christmas break—and I couldn't fail again the way I had at Northern High School. Honestly, I wasn't sure this job was the perfect fit—its students weren't as academically oriented as ones at Easton and my kids' school—but I couldn't refuse a well-paid, full-time, tenure-track position. Besides, at the interview in the two-story brick building, I got a good feeling from administrators, who had assured me students behaved well when lessons were structured. I would be taking over for Laura, who was on maternity leave until at least June, if not longer.

Yet I was struggling—and it wasn't even February.

My cheeks grew bright red, my heart pounded, but I maintained my composure. I didn't blurt out that Anne lacked manners nor mention that her parents would scold her for using foul language. Harsh words from me in this classroom of twenty-one teens would only exacerbate the problem.

"What's the problem, Anne?" I asked in English.

The classroom fell eerily silent. Constant chatter and pleas to keep quiet had been a part of the daily routine. I was center stage, the lead character in a play—was this a tragedy or a comedy? Would I captivate or alienate my audience of peer-pressured, hormone-riddled students?

"My dialogue is done," taunted Anne, a 10th grader, standing up and waving a piece of paper in front of her face. "I'm presenting it now. I'm not going to make it any longer. I stayed up late last night finishing it."

With that, she plopped down in her metal seat, looking victorious as if she had won the battle.

My face stiffened. A force too strong for me had invaded the classroom. But I was now prepared to control unruly teens after my experiences at Northern High School.

"Others haven't finished their dialogues," I said, standing proudly in front of the class. "They appreciate the extra time to work on it."

She glared at me as if I were an evil monster. "If they haven't done their dialogue, that's their problem. Just give them a zero. They know that."

I again addressed the whole class, explaining the reasons for the change in the assignment about activities they liked and disliked. They had to write ten sentences—instead of the original five—and speak for a minute. Several students had requested class time—and my assistance—to complete the assignment. I wanted everyone to do well on the dialogue. On the board, I penned a list of the order students would present. Most students look relieved and grateful—except Anne.

*"Des questions?"* I asked.

"Yes, I have a fucking question," said Anne, jumping out of her seat. "This is ridiculous. This is a joke. It's due right now, not halfway through the period."

"Watch your language. You need to calm down," I said. "Everyone should get with his or her partner. I'll come around to help each group."

My instructions were completely ignored. No one moved. Students glued their eyes on the unfolding drama near the white eraser board. Anne slouched back in her seat. I needed everyone to work—and the only way to do that was to remove Anne from the classroom.

"I'm done," said Anne. "I'm not going to write another fucking word."

*Was this her third or fourth word of profanity in the past two minutes?*

I'd had enough. She had to be squelched—otherwise, my classroom would be hell the rest of the year. I'd send her to the vice principal—they handle disciplinary issues better than me.

"You need to go to your House Office," I said. "I'll write you a pass."

Dr. Connors would speak to Anne, and then I'd write her up for using profanity. Undoubtedly, Anne would complain about how I'd changed the assignment. Perhaps I was wrong in doing this, but after my experiences at Northern, I had to listen to students' concerns about needing more help learning French. In both districts, students had had a weak foundation in French 1, partly due to incompetent teachers.

"No, I'm not fucking going anywhere," she said.

I felt like slapping her to shut her up, but teachers never do that. Beth protectively put her arms around her friend Anne's shoulders. Couldn't Beth help Anne chill, so Anne would be spared a Saturday detention or an in-school suspension?

"You must leave the room, Anne," I repeated, my voice unquivering.

She refused. I stared at her as if she were a toddler having a tantrum. The room felt too cramped for both of us as we battled for dominance of the terrain.

"I'm calling security to escort you to Dr. Connors," I said.

"Great, do that!" she bellowed. Her face flushed as she stretched out her legs as if relaxing in front of a TV.

I sensed my students' eyes following me as I walked across the room. The staccato click of my high-heeled shoes reverberated around the room. Were they shocked that I had called for help or were they pleased that I was taking charge? As I approached the phone, students murmured. The tension in the room was broken; the drama spent.

"It's fucking weird how you changed an assignment on us," Anne said. "You know I'm thinking about dropping French."

I almost blurted out "I wish you would!" But I couldn't be as free with my words as Anne was with hers. Didn't she know how the last seven French teachers had resigned or were fired in the previous two years? The world language department was widely viewed as dysfunctional. Now I was seen as the new teacher who could change that perception.

Mike, a middle-aged security guard, opened the door. "Which student should I take?"

I pointed to Anne. "Can we talk outside for a second?" I asked Mike.

I had to vent. As I told him about Anne's rude behavior, he listened patiently, unperturbed about Anne's profanity. He looked bored, as if he had seen it all. Obviously he didn't view her as the enemy. As a former cop, he'd witnessed far worse. He'd adjusted to teenagers' craziness—would I?

"You gotta go back inside," said Mike, opening the classroom door. "You can't leave them alone too long."

He summoned Anne, who begrudgingly rose from her metal perch, turning to glare at me as she trudged out the door. I watched them disappear down the long, bleak corridor.

*God, how I wish I could go home, hibernate over winter—if not longer.*

"Everybody get back to work," I said, and students—to my amazement—listened.

For the next twenty-five minutes, students rewrote and practiced their dialogues. I surveyed the room: its white walls sparkled with eye-catching posters of Paris, Quebec, and Les Emotions. Quebec beckoned me with its *"Je me souviens"* slogan; I recalled how editors had once praised me for stories written for newspapers and magazines, but now no words flowed from me. I glanced at *"Les émotions"* poster with its faces depicting *content*, *frustré* and *faché*—I was feeling frustrated, sometimes annoyed, though certainly someday I'd be happy working with teenagers. More words swirled before my eyes on the white eraser board, posters, and bookshelves, making me almost dizzy. Words, words, and more words, but my words—the ones that I'd taken pride in writing as a journalist—were no longer visible. Instead, I heard the chaotic words of teenage voices.

"Madame, could you look at my dialogue?" asked Anisha. "I think it's good."

"Read it to me," I said. "I want to listen to your pronunciation."

Anisha aimed for an A in all her classes, and as I listened to her dialogue, I thought she could master French—with my help and lots of work.

I circulated around the room; a few kind faces looked up at me and the room seemed to warm up. Don asked me to translate an English word into French. I leaned over David to tell him to change the verb tense in his dialogue—and smelled teenage sweat soaked in his sweatshirt. They welcomed my suggestions. Two students thanked me for correcting their errors. *Perhaps I am competent—and things aren't as bad as I thought.*

Other posters on the classroom's cinder block walls beckoned me. A Renoir painting of couples dancing at an outdoor café lured me back to a time in Paris when I'd felt free. As a university student, I'd leisurely sipped coffee at my neighborhood café on St. André des Arts, my main concern finishing a paper or reading a book for a French class. My mind had been opened as I roamed neighborhoods filled with scents from different times and cultures. Without children, a house and job, few responsibilities had weighed me down. Now I longed again for the freedom of those college days.

I stopped by a poster of verb conjugations, unsure if I should press down its uplifted edges. Students disliked learning grammar, much preferring fun activities like videos, games, skits, and projects.

*Should I remove the poster of the pillar verbs* être, avoir, aller, *and* faire? *No, it has to stay. It will help them learn. But how can I make them see France as exciting? Are they interested in medieval castles, purple lavender fields, and villages nestled in valleys below snow-peaked mountains? Probably not. What about seeing Monet paintings and DaVinci's Mona Lisa at the Louvre? Some might not know of these artists. I can talk about how I danced in Parisian discos while dating a French physics student. That personal story they might like. "Ooo, la, la," they'll say. "Madame was hot back then."*

"*Maintenant, vous allez présenter vos dialogues,*" I announced, halfway into the period. Students looked at me blankly. "You're going to present your dialogues now."

In groups of two, they reluctantly walked to the front of the classroom. They talked about their love of sports, friends, and music, and dislike of homework, early mornings, and work. The dialogues were understandable, though all students needed to improve pronunciation, which wasn't surprising. With their previous teacher, for months all they had done was complete packets with no speaking activities.

"*On finit les autres dialogues demain,*" I announced to bewildered faces. "We'll finish the rest tomorrow."

The bell rang. As students filed out, I stood by the door. "*Au revoir,*" I said. "*A demain.*" Monica smiled, her eyes twinkling. Anisha muttered, "Ciao, Madame." David asked if he could be the first to present his dialogue the next day. To my relief, some showed signs of appreciation. Yet I imagined others preferred chaos, which allowed them to do whatever they pleased during their hour with me. That had happened at Northern; I wouldn't let it happen here.

I returned into the quiet room bathed in sunlight with wintry rays filtering through the windows. The smells of perfume and body odor had vanished, and I rejoiced in fresh, pure air. I erased that day's lesson from the board: Had my students met the objective of knowing how to ask questions using the interrogative pronouns *qui, comment,* and *quand*? Yes, and they had completed the main activity of presenting dialogues. Most hadn't cared that the dialogues had been delayed. As teenagers, they dwelled on romance, grades, and friendships—not mastering a language or learning for learning's sake. I got that. Long ago, I had been their age.

Yet Anne's behavior bothered me. Like a bulldog, she was stubborn, willful, but generally docile, except when challenged. I felt threatened by her. I pictured her talking to administrators about my deficiencies as a teacher, and my job would be in jeopardy. To solve the problem, I vowed to listen to her concerns: Don't change assignments mid-stream. Even so, Anne still had to be written up in a disciplinary report for defiance and foul language.

As I mechanically graded French 1 quizzes, I was tempted to walk over to Dr. Connors' office to talk about Anne's behavior. But I was afraid I'd be blamed for not controlling students, as had been the case at Northern.

The door unexpectedly opened, and Vice Principal Connors walked in. She stood perfectly erect, a no-nonsense woman.

"What Anne did was wrong—and she'll be reprimanded for that," she said. "But I want you to be aware that Anne is under medication that makes her aggressive."

So, medicine to alleviate the pain of arthritis was a factor that contributed to her aggression. This partially explained her personality change. She had an IEP (Individualized Education Program), a plan listing a student's mental and physical limitations and recommending classroom accommodations. I promised to review her file. Dr. Connors encouraged me to speak to her mother.

I vowed to get to know my students better—even those I didn't like.

A few minutes later, I anxiously phoned Anne's mother, expecting her to defend her daughter.

"I'll talk to Anne about what she did," said Mrs. Schmidt. "Of course, she was out of line. The medication is to blame. At home, she sometimes lashes out at us. She'll be on the medicine another month, then she should be better."

*Wow, Anne also mistreats her parents! I didn't anticipate that.*

Later, colleagues confided in me that Anne was a big pain—even when she wasn't on medication. They advised me to show her empathy—and talk to her social worker and counselor about strategies to improve her classroom behavior.

I shouldn't let any student question my teaching abilities. Other students were saying good things about me. They were learning French. They were inspired to work hard in my classes at Harris High School.

## What Is the Student Handbook?

It serves as a guide to procedures, policies, and regulations.

It's the rule of law at school.

Teachers should study it. It's their Bible.

Students must read it to avoid getting into trouble.

Parents should know the school's rules and expectations.

## Student Handbook Contents

Students' rights and expectations.

The school's attendance, tardy, and grading policies.

Rules in classrooms, cafeteria, and stadium.

Code of conduct: Minor and major infractions.

Disciplinary actions: detention and suspensions.

Policies on fire drills, dances, and cell phone use.

## Chapter Eighteen

# NIGHTMARE

The night after first experiencing Anne's f-words in my class, I had nightmares about misplaced rosters, seating charts, and handouts. Two boys lashed out at me for putting in an incorrect grade in the grade portal. Terrified, I fled down a narrow, dark corridor, but a blockage in my path prevented my escape. A colleague begged for help photocopying quizzes. A student desperately needed directions to the nearest bathroom. An administrator notified me our meeting had been relocated to a distant room. I insisted to everyone that I couldn't tarry; I needed to get to my next class where students impatiently awaited my arrival. In a panic I ran faster, trying to get to my classroom, unsure of where it was. Each door I sprinted past resembled the last. Which one was mine? I was lost in a labyrinth of hallways, my classroom door indistinguishable from others. I screamed for help. "Where's Room 141? I've got to get there." No one would rehire a teacher who arrived in class after the bell rang. I couldn't survive without an income. "Help me, please. Someone help me."

I awoke and panic set in as I imagined foul-mouthed Anne attacking me.

★ ★ ★

The next morning, clutching my book bag and purse, I rushed down the school's main corridor of flags, clothed in a winter coat. Would my nightmare continue into the day? I certainly hoped not, but I couldn't erase the thought from my mind. I passed steel blue lockers, nervous about controlling unruly students. I needed to crack the code of working with all teens. Each step I took toward the classroom was a step toward another potential disaster.

Passing the glassed-in security booth, I spotted Mike. He was leisurely leaning back in his chair reading the newspaper while another security guard stared at a computer screen, drinking coffee. These unarmed ex-cops were not standing guard outside the fishbowl of a station; they trusted students to preserve the peace. The school, in a suburb that included Indians, Latinos, Caucasians, and African Americans abutting a wealthy district, didn't harbor gangs with concealed weapons. Nevertheless, the school district had been labeled "failing" due to low student scores on standardized tests, and a third of its students received free or reduced-cost lunch programs.

As I briskly walked toward my classroom—craving a few minutes to prepare for teaching six hours with few breaks—I dreaded a repeat of my experience at Northern, when I'd not controlled teenage defiance. I couldn't shake off worries about what Anne would do that afternoon, after the previous day's disaster. I noticed groups of students chatting with teachers; many looked relaxed as if they enjoyed school. If students didn't rebel against me, I could have a future here.

Perhaps I could identify troublemakers through what they were wearing. But most students blended in with each other by sporting jeans, sweatpants, and a t-shirt. Perhaps Anne intended to jinx me, forcing me to resign, just like students seem to have done at Northern. I imagined offering students a magic potion that turned them into perfect angels, my classroom into a monastery of learning.

A lanky boy took off his hoodie as I approached him. He didn't look evil. I reminded myself that hoodies were in style; who cared if they preferred black instead of cheerier yellow or blue? Kids just wanted to keep warm in chilly classrooms. A troublemaker could as easily wear jeans and a ragged t-shirt as sweatpants and a North Face hoodie.

I approached Vice Principal Connors, standing sentinel in the hallway near her office. "Good morning," she said.

"It's good to see you," I said. *Did she know that I'd thought about calling in sick?*

Dr. Connors resembled a nun with navy blue pants, an old-fashioned polyester jacket, and sturdy, practical loafers. She'd easily fit in at the Catholic school where I'd taught, enforcing rules fairly and consistently, intolerant of excuses.

"Good luck with Anne today," she said.

"I'm a little anxious," I said.

"That's understandable," she answered, looking at me tenderly with the eyes of an all-knowing deity. "It's not every day a student badmouths you."

"I talked to Becky last night. She made me feel better."

"She's been here a long time," she said, patting my back. "Don't hesitate to drop by my office if you need help."

Becky, my French colleague, was an organized, energetic teacher with a streak of wackiness that bordered on craziness. As a child, she'd spent years in foster homes after her mother's boyfriend had tried to burn down their home. She fended for herself, and after a divorce, she'd become even more independent, reluctant to let others take charge. I appreciated how she shared French worksheets, games, and lessons accumulated over a decade in education. I had rummaged through her filing cabinets, finding materials to make French enticing to adolescents: colorful flags from French-speaking nations, handouts on teaching reflexive verbs, Bingo games with the vocabulary of professions and parts of the body, and a DVD of French commercials. Yet before long, I had realized it was the teacher's personality and rapport with students that lead to success, not fancy materials. "Once they like you, you have it made. They'll do anything for you," a teacher once told me.

Outside my classroom, a few students loitered at their lockers, talking to friends. They huddled together and whispered in hushed tones as if conspiring to overthrow unpopular faculty members. I envisioned the unimaginable: Students running schools, as they made rules, managed classes, and got no work done. Administrators would never allow that to happen. I vowed to listen to students' concerns and attempt to adopt the district's motto of "Every child, every day."

I unlocked my classroom door, flicked on the lights, and glanced out the windows. Students streamed out of canary yellow school buses at the school's main entrance. They marched steadily forward, as if in a military parade, a patchwork of blue jeans, athletic jackets, and long coats. Some texted on their cell phones, others tuned out the world with headphones. *God, how I hope these students behave today.*

The day awakened, slowly bringing beauty for early risers, with oak trees waving their branches as if welcoming the dawn so lovely during the bleakness of winter. The sky was splatter painted a canvas of tin gray, muted salmon, and baby blue. Witnessing the day's beginning was almost magical, though that day I wouldn't have objected to *faire la grasse matinée,* sleeping late. Each morning promised so much, instilling a sense of hope in me: One teen appreciating how I made French relevant, another laughing at something I said, and a third feeling I cared for him.

*Remember how I felt to be a student! Some days I didn't want to work, other days I brimmed with energy, but all days I expected teachers to inspire.*

I had a few hours to emotionally gird myself for my next encounter with disagreeable Anne. Or perhaps I'd be lucky and she'd take off the day.

## How to Handle Profanity

Do not ignore it. Foul language isn't allowed at school.

Tell the student: "Watch your language."

React calmly. Explain profanity is unacceptable.

Give consequences matter-of-factly.

Realize students might not know what they said is offensive.

Be aware profanity is becoming more ubiquitous. Students hear it in the media and casual adult conversations.

Identify why the student used profanity.

Contact the parent if the foul language is excessive.

## Why Students Swear

To get the attention of the teacher or classmates.

To impress their peers.

To express strong emotions, such as anger or frustration.

To attack someone who hurt them.

# Chapter Nineteen

# MASTER OF MY UNIVERSE

inutes before the sixth period bell rang, Anne sauntered into the classroom, smiling as if French were her favorite class. I braced for another attack, breathing deeply to calm my rising anxiety as she approached my desk.

"I want to say I'm sorry about yesterday," she said softly.

I was stunned. *Was this really the same girl who'd lashed out at me?*

"That's okay," I said. "I understand you're taking medication."

She nodded. "It makes me angry."

No need to harbor grudges. "So, you have arthritis?"

"Yes. Can I get a hug?"

*That certainly was a change of attitude.* Unlike in other school districts, it wasn't abnormal for teachers at Harris to show affection toward students of the same sex. I reluctantly put my arms around her. "We'll start out on a new footing today," I said.

I reflected on how teenagers' moods can change radically: one day they could be ready to slash a teacher's throat, the next day offering homemade cookies and cards. Frankly, they weren't completely responsible for their outlandish behavior; their brains—specifically the prefrontal and frontal lobes—aren't yet fully developed until they're in their twenties, which explains lapses in judgment and decision-making. They cannot easily control impulses and emotions or weigh outcomes to their actions. Their brains are wired differently. No wonder they were addicted to video games and cell phones or didn't know what to do when a friend was in a drunken stupor. As a teacher, I mustn't freak out if they were disorganized, forgetful, or rude. I must also remember that I was teaching much more than French; I was helping to mold students' character as they prepared for the responsibilities of adulthood. No need to get exasperated at temporary, hotheaded behavior.

Students trickled in. A handful uttered "bonjour."

The bell rang—and the lesson began. "*Bon, on va finir les présentations de vos dialogues maintenant*," I announced, pointing to the list of students on the board. "*Voila l'ordre des dialogues. Prenez des notes—deux phrases en français par groupe*."

A few stared blankly at me. "Hey, that means we're doing the dialogues now," said Juan, loud enough for the whole class to hear. "The order is on the board. Take notes—two sentences in French per group."

Students methodically presented in front of the class—with no one mentioning the previous day's drama. Vincent, with his accent and fluency, sounded like he'd spent time in France; Birva's sentences were grammatically correct; and Claire picked up on the French intonation. I braced myself as Anne and Beth walked up to the front of the classroom, worried they'd criticize me. Instead they talked about hanging out with friends, acting in school plays, and going to the beach in summer.

"*Bon travail*," I said enthusiastically. Good work.

Only Fred, who'd been absent during the previous class, didn't present. I walked over to ask him if he needed help.

"I don't know any French," said Fred, sporting a varsity jacket with an ice hockey pin. "I didn't learn anything last year."

"Certainly you picked up some French," I said, raising my eyebrows.

"No, not really," he answered, confidently. "Hey Claire, didn't we have nine teachers over the past two years?"

*Was it really that many? I'd heard there were only seven.*

Claire, a fifteen-year-old sitting next to him, nodded. "Yah, I think that's right. My parents complained about French teachers not staying."

"So your French isn't that great?" I asked.

Fred laughed. "'Not great' would be an understatement. I can't say a word of French. Last fall, before you came, all we did was complete worksheets. Mrs. Burton would sit at her desk all period. She hated us."

I didn't ask him why; after all, I had occasionally disliked my students at Northern.

"Last year, Monsieur Pettite made anti-Semitic remarks in class one day," blurted out Claire. "You know Fred and I are Jewish."

"He got fired," added Fred. "I don't want to talk about that."

I was curious to know the details of Mr. Pettite's dismissal, but the students needed to learn the vocabulary of professions, and this discussion was off topic.

"I'm sorry to hear you lost so many teachers, but it's now

time to catch up," I said. "Everyone here can learn French. At first, I'll be translating a lot in class—that should help."

I would also review grammar and vocabulary from French 2, and present new material slower than originally planned. Thanks to my experience at Northern, I'd never rush through a curriculum again—and I would always listen to students' concerns.

"But you really don't get how little we did in class," added Fred. "It was a joke."

"Lessons are now structured so you'll learn something new every day," I said. "You'll catch up."

"I really don't get any French," said Fred, his blue eyes penetrating mine.

How sad, but was it true? Certainly he was exaggerating how little he'd learned after two years of high school French. Perhaps he had trouble speaking the language—the most difficult skill—but surely, he could read the simplest sentences.

"What was your grade in French last year?" I asked while other students listened.

"I think it was a B," he said. "Maybe one quarter it went down to a B- or C+."

"Then you understand some French."

"Don't expect us to remember stuff from last year. And don't grade us too hard."

So perhaps Harris students would work hard for good grades, which they saw as a ticket into acceptance at a decent university.

"To get a good grade, you'll have to complete all assignments—and master assessments," I said. "All of you can do that."

Evidently, Monsieur Pettite hadn't cared much about his students' education. In conversations with a colleague, I had found out how some days he played his guitar in class, jamming to Jimmy Hendrix riffs; other days, he'd yell at the students for not working. During hallway duty, he talked to colleagues about his sex life. He didn't write lesson plans until a vice principal required him to do so. For a few weeks he'd submitted plans but then stopped.

"I'm available for extra help during lunch or after school," I said. Unfortunately, few students ever took me up on this offer.

In small groups, students listed interesting professions—marine biologists, nurses, and lawyers—and why they were attracted to these jobs and where they'd get training for them. They brainstormed answers as I circulated around the room. Then the bell rang—and I truly didn't want them to leave because I actually felt needed and appreciated. I glowed as I realized I was impacting teenagers as they reflected about future careers. This is what the best teachers did day after day, shaping young people's attitudes and work ethic one student at a time. Wasn't this one of the reasons so many teachers embraced the profession? They wanted to feel they had made a difference in a person's life. And that day, I had done that for many.

★ ★ ★

I was curious about Monsieur Pettite's firing, so I asked Becky, who knew the juiciest gossip at school. Evidently Fred had criticized M. Pettite for being a bad teacher; he complained they did only writing activities, never engaging in lessons involving listening, speaking, or viewing. M. Pettite had lashed out at Fred, saying Fred thought he was better than everyone else because he was Jewish. That inspired Fred's parents to appear before the Board of Education. Soon after, Monsieur Pettite was escorted out of the building so that the district could avoid a lawsuit.

I thought about all of the public school teachers I'd known who had left the profession—Monsieur Pettite, Madame Greenbaum, and Madame Wilson—and they were just a few of the many. One-third of new teachers didn't last three years in the profession, and half of them quit after five, according to Statistics from the National Commission on Teaching and America's Future. Teachers left due to discipline issues in the classroom, unrealistic testing expectations imposed by federal legislation, and lack of mentoring by a veteran teacher. Teacher salaries in my state were high, but low wages in many states forced teachers to take second jobs.

A few years earlier, I had almost quit teaching after a particularly disastrous year. Compared to many, I had not been passionate about teaching from the start. Although, I doubted all 3.5 million teachers in America felt a calling to teach. Many could be like me: Mothers who needed to earn a living as they raise children. What other profession had similar working hours to those of school-aged children? It was time I stopped viewing my profession as key to my identity—as I had done when I was a journalist—and perceived it as a vehicle for allowing me time with my own kids.

Ten days later, on Valentine's Day, Anne again lashed out at me. So much for the respect I thought was developing between my students and me! Anne's poor behavior was almost a repeat of her previous incendiary incident—without the profanity. Anne objected to my altering an assignment by changing its point value. I explained that many students hadn't understood the homework—even after spending time on it—so I made it worth fewer points. But, she whined, she needed the points; her grade wasn't that high.

Once again, my face reddened, my heart beat faster, and everyone stopped chatting. I didn't want to call security again. How could I defuse this situation so it wouldn't end up like the previous time?

"I have to the go to the Child Study Team," Anne said suddenly, jumping out of her seat.

"Fine," I said without hesitation. Hallelujah! Good riddance! The school psychologist would soothe Anne's anxiety. "Before you go, look at the board so you know what we're doing today and write down the homework."

The situation was resolved. I needed to figure out how best to control this type of situation. It was time to return to the lesson; administrators always frowned on downtime, preaching "Keep them busy" and "Don't let them get off task." But where had I put the corrected version of the homework assignment? On the Elmo projector? My desk? My clipboard? No, it had disappeared. Had Anne or another student snatched it? I couldn't waste time searching for it. Quick! Improvise! I asked a student to write answers on the board. No need to write mine. Later that day, I found my homework handout underneath a stack of quizzes on the counter behind my desk. I made a note to be more organized.

Priyal, a girl with a mischievous streak, volunteered, and I breathed a sigh of relief. I could count on students to help me out. She probably wanted to separate herself from chatty peers, so she could earn an A. I liked her. She made me feel as if I were helping her succeed.

As students copied the answers on the board, I felt that I was again master of my universe of teens, some intolerable, some kind—just like adults. I regained a semblance of composure, pointing out the verbs in the *passé composé* and *imparfait*. Together we translated sentences. "*Joan d'Arc avait 13 ans quand elle a entendu des voix qui lui ont dit d'aider Charles VII et son armée.*" Joan of Arc was thirteen years old when she heard voices telling her to help Charles VII and his army.

Joan of Arc was privy to whispers of actions she believed were necessary to save France—and she heeded these words. She was a real heroine in France's history. What were my inner voices telling me? Leave teaching? I'd already applied to half a dozen jobs in communications, just in case Laura didn't return from maternity leave, though rumor had it that Laura was happy taking care of her twin boys and didn't want to teach full time in a district far from home.

I missed my former job as a reporter, where every day I'd discovered something new about our world while meeting new and fascinating people. As a journalist, I knew exactly what I was doing, while as teacher, I still wasn't confident I was doing it right.

But part of me wanted to continue working at a public school with its decent salary and medical insurance. I was feeling better about Harris students, and so far, no writing jobs I'd applied for had resulted in an interview. Perhaps it was time to turn teaching French into a job I liked. Could I tap my creativity and have fun at school? Maybe I could teach students how to report and write a story—in French!

My French 3 kids needed a quick review of the past tense—even if they hated grammar. "Look again at the sentences about Joan of Arc," I instructed, pointing to the screen. "Why are some in the *passé compose* and others the *imparfait*? Remember what I told you yesterday?"

For a minute students stared at the board; some eyes showed comprehension.

Ratika raised her hand, her silky hair tumbling down her back. "The *passé compose* is used when something happens quickly. And the *imparfait* is when you regularly do something."

"Excellent," I said proudly. "Can you give me an example?"

She consulted her notebook. "Like I used to play with dolls—that would be the *imparfait*. The *passé compose* is something like, I went to the store yesterday."

I felt like high fiving her.

"Think about what you used to do. Play with cars? Jump rope?" I asked. "Make three sentences about these activities. Remember to use the *imparfait*. You can work with a partner."

They rejoiced, relishing time with partners they chose—their friends. I was improving at the art of teaching, even if Anne disagreed. As I listened to their answers, I pondered my mistakes at Northern: I had been too critical and impatient with my students, and I didn't show I cared enough about them or listen to them. I had forgotten how demanding it is to learn a language. But that day, Joan of Arc had saved me. I thought about her power to hear The Divine, and that had helped me tap into my own ability to listen to the truth about teaching. I was beginning to blossom as a teacher. I had to cast aside doubt about my abilities to reach teenagers and stop thinking negatively about this noble profession.

## Characteristics of Good Teachers

Non-combative and consistent

Clear expectations

Patient and creative

Well-organized and fair

Few referrals for disciplinary issues

## Chapter Twenty

# FOREIGN FLAGS

During my hall duty, I sat at a desk in the school's main corridor. This one-hour break from teaching provided time to get work done. I started grading quizzes, but the dozens of flags hanging overhead distracted me. I glanced up at the flags honoring students' countries of origin, their bright colors reminding me of a time when I had travelled the world.

I set aside my red pen, looking for flags of countries where I'd once lived: Morocco, Sweden, Switzerland, and Egypt. I spotted Morocco's red flag with a green star. It was motionless in this cavernous, bright hallway. But, as a child, I remembered how the Moroccan flag on our car waved, a chauffeur driving my sister and me to school. As a diplomat's daughter, I led a privileged life in a developing country, with housekeepers, private schools, and a house with a pool and tennis courts. While living abroad, it was normal for State Department employees to have such amenities. I never thought then about finding the right career or partner. How carefree I had been. I questioned whether I should tell my students about my childhood. Would they find my life interesting, or would they see me as elitist?

A willowy girl chewing gum walked by my desk, drawing me out of my reverie. I asked her for a pass. "No one checks hall passes," she said, reluctantly showing me her planner. "Why do you?"

A few years earlier her attitude would have annoyed me, but now I took it in stride. No need to get flustered by teenagers. She didn't mean any harm.

I tried to get back to grading French quizzes, but before long, my eyes darted back to the flags, particularly ones from Ecuador, Haiti, and India, the homeland of some of my students. What had their lives been like before moving to America? Did their parents speak English, or did they act as translators? Some might have fled political repression, still haunted by turmoil in their home countries, worried about the safety of relatives left behind. Other families had realized financial success, undoubtedly after working hard for years. Were these students torn between two cultures? I wanted to find out more about them. The flags coaxed me to understand my students even better.

A middle-aged history teacher approached me. I recognized him from our faculty meetings. "So, how's it going? I'm sitting over there," said Bob Lund, pointing to a chair down the hallway. "I have hall duty too."

I spoke to him about Anne. He recommended I not take it seriously. "You never know what's happening in teenagers' lives," he said calmly. "They could be dealing with some serious stuff. Just see if you can make them laugh in class. A little humor can make their day."

I admitted that I didn't often lighten up in class.

"It will come," he said. "They're just seeing what you're made of. You haven't been here long enough for them to trust you. Give it time. Talk to Anne's Child Study Team. They'll give you insight about how to work with her."

"How long will it take for me to relax in class?" I asked.

"The first year is tough . . . really tough," he said. "Then it gets easier. I've been here so long that I'm on autopilot."

The good news, I told him, was that some students had warmed up to me.

"Sounds like you're getting there," said Bob. "Kids want teachers to tell them some personal stuff, but not too much. I should get back to my station."

My students already knew I had three children and two cats. I hadn't mentioned my sons were born in Switzerland and my daughter in Sweden, but now among such an international crowd, maybe I could. I would tell them about growing up in Casablanca where, without knowing much French, I'd been thrust into a classroom full of Moroccan children.

My students might be open to hearing about my first teaching experience as a Peace Corps volunteer in Niger, a landlocked, West African nation. In a dusty town with few paved roads, I taught middle school English with no textbook or electronics. I studied Hausa, a tribal language, and befriended United Nations road-builders and Canadian priests and nuns. My home had running water and electricity, but no phone or indoor toilet. I counted the weeks left *en poste* by the number of pink malaria pills remaining in a bottle on my kitchen shelf. Certainly, my students would be intrigued about the two years I taught in one of the world's poorest countries.

Momentarily, I reflected on my connections with students. The previous fall, in another district, an eighth grade student had criticized me for being distant. In that English class, the kids had been learning new vocabulary words, one of which was "aloof." "That's you, Mrs. Nelson," he'd said. "You don't show much feeling and you don't get involved with us." Wow! That hit me hard! After that comment, I knew I'd have to change. I'd need to be more approachable and friendly, like I'd been at the prep and parochial schools. This would guarantee success at this public school as well.

I finished grading my French 1 quizzes. My star pupils Dhruv and Maggie earned As, most students got Bs and Cs, and two students failed. The grades were evenly distributed; the average score 76 percent. Enough students had mastered the material to make it clear I'd taught it properly. If the average had been 70 percent or below, I would have thrown out the quiz and retaught the lesson. What a long way I'd come since Northern when most of my French 2 students had failed assessments. How proud I now felt!

In glass cases in the hall I eyed rows of trophies, a shrine to the school's star athletes, who had won regional and state championships. I walked over to a case, peering at a gold trophy of a basketball player reaching out his arms to catch a ball, the moment of victory frozen in time. I wanted to be recognized as contributing to the school's excellence. It was time I focused less on the past and more on the present. I promised myself to get involved with students. I would help turn Harris into a more intellectual institution, like schools in the neighboring district, by putting more rigor in my French classes. I'd already told students not to think of themselves as the poorer, less fortunate cousin of students in that wealthy district. My students were just as capable and hardworking, and their economic status shouldn't affect the pursuit of their dreams.

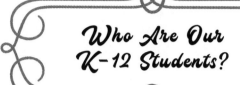

## Who Are Our K-12 Students?

**White: 45.8%**

**Hispanic: 28.0%**

**Black: 15.0%**

**Asian: 5.4%**

**Two or more races: 4.5%**

**American Indian/Alaska Native: 0.9%**

**Pacific Islander: 0.4%**

*Source: National Center for Education Statistics (2020)*

## What Kind of Child Succeeds at School?

Respects authority

Gets along with fellow students

Lives with a stable family

Interacts with responsible adults

Feels a sense of hope

## Chapter Twenty-One

# CONFERRING WITH A COLLEAGUE

For two nights I lost sleep over an impending meeting with Anne, her mother, and Anne's Child Study Team counselor. I expected to be blamed for Anne's distaste for French. To top it off, I was anxious about my future: Laura might return from maternity leave to reclaim her job in September. I sought comfort from my colleague Becky, who also taught French.

After school I walked into Becky's room, glancing at oak desks that resembled ones from classrooms a century ago. I pictured scholars analyzing Montaigne's essays or silently reading chapters of Victor Hugo's *Les Misérables*. Perhaps Becky's students had become fluent while studying in these old fashioned desks, just like my prep school students had done around an oval mahogany table. There, a dozen students had discussed in French the merits and flaws of *The Count of Monte Cristo.*

The dimmed lights in Becky's room promoted calm; I made a note to turn off some lights in my room. Near Becky's windows, students' folders were stacked with their prized work. In contrast, my room next door featured no neat folders, and metal desks were scattered haphazardly after students had moved them to work on dialogues with friends. I should have reminded them to straighten them up afterward—next time!

That February day, Becky was staring at her computer screen as if deciphering an encrypted secret code. I almost left, but I needed answers. During the day, she frantically rushed around the school, clutching handouts, her shoulder length blond hair perfectly in place. Often she barely muttered "hi" to me; occasionally I warranted a "I can't talk today." In May, once she finished graduate school to become a supervisor, she promised she'd have more time to chat.

"What's up?" she said, looking up from her screen.

I stood behind her, eyeing a half-written email on her computer. "Do you know Anne Schmidt?" I asked.

"I never had her," she answered, resuming typing. "But I've heard other teachers say she's a bitch."

"She used the f-word to me," I said.

That got her attention; she stopped writing. "Don't take it personally. It happened to me as well. It's a shock. Just don't let it get you down."

"She apologized the next day," I added.

"So you see. Nothing to worry about," she said, returning to her email.

That's the moment when I should have left; she'd given me a vote of confidence.

"I don't know if I fit in here," I said softly. "No one ever swore at me like that."

Becky flashed an expression of disbelief. "Of course you do. You're taking this job seriously, which your predecessors didn't. The students are warming up to you. So what's the problem?"

"I miss my days writing," I admitted.

Becky glared at me as if I were a truant toddler needing a stern reprimanding. I felt her frustrations. How many previous French teachers had griped about working at the school?

"So do your writing on the side—or during the summer. Nothing's stopping you from that."

She was right. I shouldn't complain. I just needed to balance writing with teaching. I would commit to carving out an hour each day for writing, penning it on my schedule. It would become a class I couldn't skip.

"By the way, I'm meeting Anne's child study person and mom tomorrow. They might think I'm responsible for Anne's behavior."

Becky straightened up in her swivel chair. "Relax. You'll be fine. The school isn't out to get you. Just mention strategies about how to improve. That's it."

Becky's words were encouraging. I didn't need to worry. Like me, she'd switched professions in her 40s, giving up a sales career to teach. In her first years in the classroom, she couldn't wait to get to middle school to teach units on the family, home, and food. She created her own materials, cramming in lots of activities so kids wouldn't get bored.

Now, she was the last one to leave school in the afternoon and often came in Saturday to prepare lessons. She prided herself on being a hard worker, almost resenting anyone who did less than her. Later, I realized she used school as a haven where she temporarily forgot her personal problems. Work partially alleviated her loneliness of being divorced. But her grown disabled son, who lived at home, made the house less silent, the nights less dark.

At Harris, I didn't need to put in sixty-hour work weeks like Becky, but I could be as effective as she was. I was getting quicker at writing lessons plans, completing professional development workshops, and grading. On average, I spent forty hours on schoolwork. I got my job done during the workday, leaving afternoons and evenings for other pursuits. That's when I'd find a few hours to pen my thoughts, at night, when silence reigned, and my children slept soundly in their beds.

A typical teacher works fifty-four hours a week—just under half that time is devoted to teaching.

*Source: EducationWeek*

**What Takes Time Outside the Classroom?**

Planning lessons

Grading

Communicating with parents

Handling discipline issues

Collaborating with colleagues

Attending school meetings

Fulfilling professional development requirements

Helping students during free periods or lunch

## Chapter Twenty-Two

# WHY CAN'T I SHUT UP?

The next day I vowed to get to know my French 3 students better by chatting with them as they left the room, complimenting them on their fluency in French. I stopped Dan, a burly brunette, as he exited.

"*Bon travail aujourd'hui*," I said, as other teens filtered past us. Good work today.

"*Merci*," he answered.

"Who did you have for French last year?" I asked, almost certain he had Becky, not a multitude of teachers.

"I was in school in California. I've only been here since September."

Neither of us had a long history at Harris High School, though after six months, Dan was well-adjusted with good friends, including Anne. Perhaps he could provide advice on how to squelch Anne's emotional outbursts.

"By the way, do you know what's bothering Anne?" I asked. "She seems annoyed."

He shrugged, lowering his intense, penetrating eyes. We were alone. "She's sometimes moody."

"She's tough to handle. It doesn't make it easy to teach class."

He fidgeted, as if he didn't want to hear a teacher's feelings about his friend.

"She's not that bad; she actually works in your class."

He was right about that; she finished assignments. "I'm tired of all the chitchat."

"We're not that bad," he said. "Your class is right after lunch. We haven't yet finished conversations with friends."

I had never thought about that. "It's sometimes still loud," I said. "I wish it was quieter. Sometimes I feel as if I'm wasting my time teaching French. Maybe I should do something else. I like to write—maybe I should do that."

Dan stared at me; his chestnut brown eyes quizzical as if this secret was too much to handle. A few long seconds passed. Why was I admitting to a student I wanted to be somewhere else besides school?

I had viewed Dan as a sympathetic, artistic student, who'd empathize with my desire to write. He was an actor, someone who needed to express himself creatively like me. But to deepen relationships with students, I should focus on *their* interests, not *mine*. I should have asked him about his role in the upcoming school musical or his adjustment to the East Coast.

"But we get work done," he said, almost in a whisper. "We behave better with you than with the teacher last fall."

"Yes, I heard she wasn't active in the classroom."

"I'm getting used to your teaching style. It's different from my teacher in California, but I'm learning a lot."

*My God, students knew about different teaching styles! What was mine? What was the norm? Until I became a teacher, I'd never heard about teaching styles.*

"Thanks, Dan. I'm glad you're in my class," I said. "Don't mention to Anne that we talked, okay?"

He nodded. I watched as he walked away, his tall, solid body visible among a wave of adolescents.

Damn. I should not have discussed my problems with Dan. What a complete idiot I was! I only wanted affirmation it was okay to be artistic, and I mistakenly believed Dan would do this. What a *faux pas*! I closed my eyes as I prayed Dan wouldn't tell others about our conversation.

Drained, I couldn't face my students the following day, so I decided to call in sick, justifying it as a mental health day. To prepare for my absence, I headed to the faculty room to make photocopies of worksheets for the substitute teacher.

Mary, the veteran English teacher, stopped me in the hallway to ask how it was going. I told her a few kids were acting up. She joined me in the privacy of the faculty room where I confessed my classes weren't as orderly as I would have liked.

"The students are testing you—and they will for the rest of the year," said Mary, who was nearing retirement. "It won't be easy, but when you come back next year, it will be a whole different experience. You do want job options this fall, don't you?"

The history teacher had said the same thing. What was it about first-year teachers at public schools? Did students see their anxiety and lack of confidence and decide to take advantage of this? Perhaps teachers who had majored in education were better prepared to handle the first nine months in a district. I'd not struggled at Sacred Heart as a newbie, but public schools were a whole different beast.

Her eyes showed kindness and concern. "What can I do to improve?" I asked.

"From what I hear, you're doing okay," she said. "Students aren't complaining about you. They're saying you make them work—not like your predecessors."

★ ★ ★

Two mornings later, as I drove to work, the sky transformed from a tin gray into a tableau of pinks, oranges, and red. The world was ablaze, as if the universe were advocating a new beginning, the end of darkness. My spirits were uplifted. I'd thought about the challenges of teaching in public schools and surmised that it might have to do with how students are parented. Some parents favored diligence and discipline; others just wanted their child to graduate. This blending of different values made it tough to lead a class. Should teachers focus on high achievers, low ones, or the mean? Harris's motto was Every Child, Every Day. So I had to make sure all my students learned something no matter the parental involvement. If I accepted these differences, I would be okay. Simple solution.

Besides, on my day at home, I realized how solitary life could be, though I'd written a bit, which always made me feel balanced.

In the hallway near my classroom, I stopped to talk to Rajveer, one of my students, about what had happened on my day off.

"In study hall in the cafeteria, a teacher told Juan, Ben, and Sean to stop goofing off in French, and start working," she said. "She said they'd be in big trouble if they gave the teacher a hard time."

"Who was the teacher?" I asked.

She didn't know. I wanted to thank her for intervening.

Later I discovered it was Julie, a no-nonsense woman who maintained, even on bad days, she'd never leave Harris High School. She told me how a student the previous day had bragged, "We got rid of another French teacher."

Julie and I laughed about how shocked he must have been to see me in class the next day.

"Thanks for your help," I said.

"They can't mess with you," she responded. "If they do, they'll hear from me." My heart burst with gratitude: Teachers cared about me, and I could depend on them. That gave me the confidence I needed to face Anne, her mother, and the Child Study Team at the upcoming meeting. No way would it be a repeat of the meeting at Northern with Meghan, her mother, and my supervisor.

## No-Nos for Teachers

Beware the teachers' lounge. You'll hear colleagues' complaints and gossip.

Don't be a friend to your students. They need a teacher, not a buddy.

Don't badmouth your district. Comments could get back to your boss.

Don't share too much information about yourself to students. Private matters should remain private.

Don't tell students how you feel about their peers. You should respect and get along with all students.

## Chapter Twenty-Three

# WHO IS THE HEROINE?

The next day during my free period I met Anne, her mother, and Betsy, the Child Study Team counselor. In an airless cubicle of a room, Anne slouched in her chair while Betsy read a document outlining Anne's medical and psychological issues. Her mother had dark circles under her eyes. Had she suffered sleepless nights, anxious about her out-of-control daughter? I'd used concealer to hide bags under my eyes, the result of fitful sleep. I fretted Anne knew about the incident with Dan and she would hold that against me.

"Let's see, Anne, how we can help you achieve the best possible results in school," said Betsy, a perky, blond-haired professional in her twenties. "I understand you had some problems in French recently."

I kept nervously quiet. I'd committed a blunder by confessing private and personal information to Dan, a student friend of Anne's. Had he communicated to Anne some of what I revealed to him about her?

"Madame Nelson always changes assignments," said Anne, in a skin-tight t-shirt. "It's annoying. It's not fair when I already did the work, and just want to present and I can't."

On her laptop, Betsy took notes. I felt as if I were in a courtroom, but certainly I would be allowed to defend myself.

Anne's mother interjected. "Let's take it easy, Anne."

"Yes, that can be frustrating," said Betsy calmly. "So you finished the work at home, and then in class you were given more time, right?"

Anne nodded and glared at me. "It's weird changing due dates," said Anne. "I shouldn't have stayed up late finishing it. Next time, I won't."

Betsy asked me to explain why I'd changed the assignment. "I'm thinking of what benefits all students," I said. "I'm new here. I'm figuring out students' ability in French. Sometimes, it's necessary to give them more time to learn what they didn't learn last year."

Betsy nodded in approval. She embraced the school's rule of ensuring that every child learned every day, and that flexibility was necessary in teaching. "That sounds fine, but I understand why Anne had objections to it."

Mrs. Schmidt, a middle-aged woman with streaks of gray in her shoulder-length hair, sighed, frowning as if she was aware of how Anne didn't see all perspectives of a situation. When and how was empathy learned?

"It's the medicine she was on," she said. "It makes her angry sometimes. Now, fortunately, she's off it."

Perhaps then Anne would turn into a lamb from a lion. What a relief that Mrs. Schmidt supported me, and no one seemed to know about my conversation with Dan.

"I agree with Anne that I should try to be more rigid about due dates," I admitted sheepishly. "Once I get to know students' capabilities, I will do that."

Anne grinned victoriously.

"I checked the grade portal, and it seems Anne is doing fine in French," Betsy said.

Anne didn't react to this information. I was surprised she

didn't blurt out that she had better get an A in the class because she was working hard and was smart.

"I'm pleased with Anne's performance," I added. "She seems to get the material. She's a very capable student with great potential."

Anne straightened up in her chair and smiled after the two compliments. "Sometimes it's not easy for us," said Anne politely. "The old teacher was terrible. We didn't learn much French."

"Let's see what else we need to discuss," said Betsy, looking down at her paper. "You just got off the medication for arthritis last week, right?"

"But I'll have to take it again in another month or so," said Anne.

"Dr. Connors resolved the issue about the use of profanity in the classroom, right?" asked Betsy.

Anne lowered her eyes, as if embarrassed. "Yes, I shouldn't have said that."

How fortunate that administrators at this school took student misbehavior seriously. Betsy took some time to type notes on her laptop. Anne looked bored, fiddling with her hair. Mrs. Schmidt scrolled on her phone. The silence made me feel awkward as if I didn't have anything to say to a student with whom I had already spent several months. I needed to create a friendly atmosphere, so I brought up what we'd been studying in French class.

"You seemed to like the lesson on Joan of Arc," I said.

Anne nodded, looking straight at me. "Yeah, it was okay."

"I can't believe a teenager led an army to battle," I said. "How courageous is that?"

"She was awesome," said Anne brightly. "Teenagers don't do that type of stuff. It's freaking terrible she died."

"But because of her actions, she became a heroine," I said.

During that short conversation, I established a connection with Anne; our rapport felt natural, no longer strained.

"Well, it sounds like French class interests you," piped in Betsy. "And we've made some progress today resolving issues between you and Mrs. Nelson. You can go back to class, Anne. It was also a pleasure to meet you, Mrs. Schmidt."

Anne grabbed her Hello Kitty backpack, slinging it over her shoulder. Mrs. Schmidt thanked us for our time. "If I have any questions, I'll email you or Mrs. Nelson," she said, as she exited.

I was antsy to leave and shout for joy that no one had brought up my conversation with Dan. But Betsy hadn't dismissed me yet.

"That was a very productive meeting," she said jovially. "I'm glad Mrs. Schmidt is so rational about her daughter's behavior. It sounds like you picked up strategies to help in the classroom with Anne."

I felt grateful for Dan's discretions and proud of his maturity. I had learned from my mistakes, understanding that I should never confide in a student about a personal issue, especially one related to a fellow teenager or my job at school. My confidence was growing that I could manage teenagers, even if I still had a lot to learn. I reassured myself Dan would keep our secret; undoubtedly, he was thinking about his personal issues, not mine.

Days later, a French 2 student asked me if I was French, since I didn't have an accent when speaking French. Now was a good time to reveal more about myself by telling them about my childhood in Morocco. Certainly, Mr. Lund was right that students appreciated knowing some personal information about adults with whom they spent so much time.

I explained that I spent three years at a French Catholic school in Casablanca, Morocco. I was seven years old, too young to be sent with my brothers to the boarding school in Tangier. No international or American school existed where I lived. So, six hours every day, I heard only French.

"Really?" asked Rohan, wide-eyed. "No one spoke English?"

"My sister did," I said. "But she was in kindergarten, so I never saw her."

The students laughed and I relaxed. "How did you understand what the teacher was saying?" asked Sarah, a petite, strawberry-blond ninth grader.

"At first I didn't," I answered. "But by Christmas, I got it. It's easy to pick up a new language when you're that young and exposed to immersion."

From their faces, I saw disbelief as if I'd assigned them Stendhal's *Le Rouge et Le Noir* to read for homework. Some struggled to learn a dozen new vocabulary words in a week, so how could their teacher pick up a whole language in a matter of months, at less than half their age? I explained that initially I had to work hard to understand simple conversations. But after hundreds of hours in the classroom, I began to achieve fluency. I reminded my students that the secret to success is hard work, and lots of time for studying.

"Wait, didn't you learn some French before school started?" interjected Natalie, the class artist.

"During the summer I had a few French lessons, but that was it. There was no ESL program like here."

"Did you have any friends?" asked Sarah, her braces gleaming. "Cuz if you didn't know French, no one would like you."

I'd forgotten how paramount friendships were to teenagers: It was their BFFs, best friends forever, with whom they confided their inner secrets, with parents often clueless about what they were really thinking.

"At first, I had only a few American friends from the expat

community," I said. "But once I spoke French, I made friends at school."

Students stared at me in wonderment. Did they think it was bizarre to have such an experience in childhood? I didn't see it as weird; it was part of being raised in an exotic place with no American schools. Like me, two of my brothers had learned French when my parents had been posted to Tunisia, attending French schools in Tunis.

I listened to my students as they chatted among themselves. "Man, that's wild." "I don't want to go to a school where I can't understand anyone." "I wished I learned French as a kid. Then this class would be so easy."

They were truly engaged in class today, and for a few minutes, they explored how their childhoods in New Jersey had vastly differed from mine. Not one of them had been required to learn another language in a foreign country, even though some of their parents had grown up abroad. Students from Ecuador, Senegal and Haiti remarked about their families' origins and integration into American life. All were discussing what it meant to be an American. I'd finally earned students' respect, another breakthrough.

All was going so well. Yet what would happen in September? I felt anxious thinking about how Laura might return from maternity leave and want her job back. I couldn't take starting over in a new school district. It was hard putting down roots at a new school, and this was my third time doing it. But I took consolation in how earlier that spring I had applied to several journalism and communication jobs—just in case Laura wanted her job back.

## Resources for Students with Special Needs

Teachers refer students with social, emotional, academic, or medical issues to a local school team known as the Child Study Team (CST). In some states, this team is known as the Pupil Personnel Team (PPT) or School Building Level Committee (SBLC).

To qualify for services, a child must have at least one of thirteen conditions covered under the Individuals with Disabilities Education Act (IDEA). These include dyslexia, ADHD, autism, bipolar disorder, schizophrenia, depression, speech impairment, blindness, deafness, and below average intellectual ability.

The team develops an Individualized Education Program (IEP), which lists accommodations to support the child. This can include anything from assistive technology tools and preferential seating in class to extended time on tests and having questions read orally.

A child with a mental or physical impairment that limits major life activities can qualify for a 504 plan. These plans support students with issues such as impulsivity, hyperactivity, low self-esteem, sustaining attention, and poor organizational skills. These plans, named after Section 504 of the Rehabilitation Act of 1973, are less extensive than an IEP.

## Chapter Twenty-Four

# IS MOVING AN OPTION?

In my home office, I scanned through emails, zeroing in on one from the University of Virginia, expecting another rejection. I clicked on the email with the subject line "Senior Writer Position."

"Would you be kind enough to forward several of your writing samples?" wrote Tim, the editor of the alumni magazine for the university's business school.

I felt like jumping out of my seat, racing around the house, yelling to the world that somebody still thought of me as a journalist. Not to mention that someone was an editor at a prestigious university. Within minutes I shot back an email, attaching stories I'd written as a freelancer.

That weekend as I folded laundry, I simulated an interview, developing answers to questions Tim might ask me. While grocery shopping I contemplated living in Charlottesville, a hot spot for retirees, and while cooking dinner, I thought how happy I'd be working again in a quasi-newsroom. Yet a large part of me questioned whether I should even consider leaving my job and home in New Jersey. Teaching no longer frazzled me, and my children were settled in our suburban neighborhood.

It wasn't worth getting worked up about a job that might not happen. Undoubtedly dozens of candidates were vying for the job, and Tim might find my clips dated or dry. I dampened my optimism about progressing to the next stage.

On Monday afternoon, I opened an email from Tim. "Your clips are very nice. Is there a time when I could call you in the next few days?"

Way to go! An interview! I did a happy dance in front of my computer. I immediately responded to the email, then ran downstairs to the kitchen. "Patrick, Emily, Nicholas," I called out. "I need to talk to you guys."

Patrick was snacking at the kitchen table, hungry after his football workout. Nicholas was rummaging through the fridge after tennis practice, while Emily studied European history on the couch in the family room.

"Hey, I'm going to be interviewing for a writing job," I announced.

"You'd like that," said Patrick, biting into a chocolate donut. "All you do upstairs is write."

"Where's the job?" asked Nicholas.

*Did I really have to answer that?*

"The University of Virginia in Charlottesville," I said gingerly.

Nicholas slammed the fridge door shut, Patrick stopped eating his donut, and Emily looked up from her textbook, a little smile on her face. "Momio, you're going to follow me to college."

That September, Emily would study business at James Madison University in Harrisonburg, Virginia, while Nicholas would be a junior in high school and Patrick a sophomore. I anticipated the boys wouldn't want to leave our home, unwilling to sever connections with friends from elementary school.

Nicholas walked over to the kitchen table, a glass of Coke in his hand. "Does this mean if you get the job we'll move to Virginia?"

*Staying behind with their father was an option, but I wanted to be a part of their last years in high school.*

"Yes, we'd all go to Virginia," I said.

"I'd be okay if there's football there," said Patrick, retrieving some orange juice from the fridge.

Trust Patrick to focus on what made him happy: football. "I looked into that. The high school in Charlottesville has a very good football program," I said. "Down south, they really love football."

Nicky looked annoyed, as if he'd just lost hundreds of points playing a video game. "I don't like the idea of moving away. I'd miss my friends."

I hadn't thought through what their reaction would be to this. I began to regret telling them so impulsively. Instead I should have called a girlfriend, who would have shared my excitement, possibly suggesting ways to gently break the news to my kids. I had to remember that my children had spent their entire childhood here, while I'd moved every two or three years in my childhood. I was used to saying goodbye to friends; they weren't. Plus, they were only a few years away from going to college.

"Let's see what happens with the interview," I told Nicholas. "I might not get the job, and even if I do, maybe you could live with Dad."

"I'm not going to move, Mom," said Nicholas, emphatically. "That's it."

"Okay, Nicky," I said. "At least I know what you think about Virginia."

"Dad won't like it either," he murmured, walking out of the kitchen. "He's going to be so pissed off at you."

I grew up among restless nomads. My parents viewed moving as an adventure: We climbed the Giza pyramids; hiked rambling trails where Wordsworth reflected on nature; and saw Shakespearean plays at Stratford's Globe Theater. I loved the novelty of living in new places and getting to know people of different cultures. Nevertheless, I began to feel like a chameleon, who constantly changed its color to blend in. I superficially fit in everywhere, but nowhere deeply.

"I'll talk to Dad," I said. "We could make it work."

Over the years, the anger of the divorce had been replaced with a strong friendship. My ex-husband dropped by for dinner weekly, and we regularly talked on the phone. We celebrated Thanksgiving and Christmas as a family, realizing we needed each other's help raising our children. No doubt about it: Henrik would hate me for leaving him alone in New Jersey without his sons for companionship.

The following two days, I read through the University of Virginia's business school's magazine, finding it neither too radical nor too artistic. I pictured myself writing stories about alumni managing non-profits, students studying abroad, and professors discussing Fed policy. My children and I would live in a house near campus, and they'd take the train to see their father every two weeks. Yet they might forbid me from taking the job if I were offered it.

That Thursday afternoon, I ordered my three children to be quiet for fifty minutes: They mustn't yell out when dinner would be ready or argue among themselves. A few minutes before 4 p.m., I locked the office door. To calm my nerves, I paced the room and breathed in deeply. *If it's meant to be, it will be.*

Finally the phone rang, and Mr. Matsiano's soothing voice put me at ease. I felt as if I were catching up with an old friend. I liked this guy. Was he married? Come on, what was I thinking? It was a job interview, not a date!

I explained how I could put my MFA to use as I wrote for the magazine using literary techniques. The program was worth the time and money. We discussed the types of stories I would be writing, the university's culture, and the cohesiveness of the small staff. His job wasn't all consuming, allowing him time to pursue outside interests, such as biking and travelling.

"Well, I enjoyed talking with you," he said, after an hour. "I have several other interviews next week, but you're a top candidate. I'll be making a quick decision."

*Wow, I was a finalist! Couldn't he just hire me on the spot? Yet, that would create a rift in my family.*

"UVA sounds like a wonderful place to work," I said. "Thanks for interviewing me."

"I'll be in touch soon. I'm going on vacation right after Memorial Day, and I want this taken care of by then."

That night, Henrik came by the house to give Emily two *Wall Street Journal* articles about finance and marketing in preparation for her business school studies that fall. I invited him to stay for dinner, and as we gathered around a table on the deck, I announced that I was a finalist for the job in Virginia. They all stared at me as if I had metamorphosed into a family-bashing monster.

Patrick was the only one who congratulated me. "I don't mind moving. You said there's a good football team there, right?"

I nodded. Everyone stopped eating.

"Don't you understand that I like it here?" said Nicholas, his voice faltering. "I don't want to leave in my junior year."

Their father, who resembled Cary Grant though with sloping shoulders, was livid. "You're going to take my kids away from me. You can't do that."

"You can see them every other weekend," I said. "There's a train every day. Or I could drive them halfway to you."

"My whole life will change without them," he said, his neck flushing red. "It's not right for you to do this."

"We can make it work," I said. "It's not a bad time to leave. Nicholas has two years of high school left, and Patrick three. Besides, my high school might not rehire me."

"It's not good for kids to move," said Henrik, his eyes sad. "They need stability. They won't do well if they're taken out of a place they're used to."

"Well, what about me? That's all I did when I was growing."

"That explains why you're so weird, Mom," joked Emily.

They all knew how, as a child, I'd attended seven schools in five countries over thirteen years.

"And look how you turned out, Mom," said Nicholas angrily. "You don't have many friends. You're crazy to think about moving all of us."

*That really hurt! Why did he have to be as snarky as some of my students? Confident, cool dude, I-can-take-anything Nicholas felt his life would be ruined if we left our colonial home in the valley.*

"But Nicky, this job will allow me to return to journalism," I said forcefully. "It's something that I trained for and would really enjoy."

"Mom, you can't just think of yourself," said Nicholas. "What about us? Don't you care about us?"

That's when I blew up.

"Listen, you guys," I said angrily. "I've made so many sacrifices for you. I've maintained the upkeep on this super huge house after your father moved out so that you could continue attending the same school. I left the newspaper job to spend more time with you. I tried to make teaching work. Don't you understand that maybe it's time for me to follow *my* dreams? Can't I ever be selfish?"

My children looked stunned.

"But Mom, don't you like it here?" asked Patrick timidly.

"Oh, honey," I said. "I love it here with all of you."

Henrik got up from his chair and started pacing the deck. "Do you want to destroy my relationship with them?" said Henrik, his voice quivering. "I won't ever see them."

"Of course you'll see them," I said. "It just won't be as often."

Henrik paused at the railing, gazing out at the sloping yard bordered by shadowing trees. He rubbed his face with his hands.

"Virginia is way too far away," said Henrik. "The divorce agreement says that you'll stay close by so that I can see the kids regularly. That won't happen now."

Nicholas interrupted his father. "Mom, don't you get it? I have lots of friends here. Mike, Xavier, Benny. I don't want to leave them. I like it here. Can't you find a job at a university nearby?"

"Princeton doesn't want to hire me," I said, sighing. "Virginia is the only place interested in me."

For a moment, Nicholas and Henrik were silent, their food untouched. Patrick gobbled down his chicken and rice, while Emily finished her corn, unfazed. The tension had mostly dissipated, but Henrik still looked mad.

"Can't you just wait a few more years until they are all out of high school?" asked Henrik.

"There might not be a job for me then."

Henrik didn't speculate on job prospects in three years.

"Just teach at Harris for a while," said Nicholas. "It wasn't bad for you this year."

"Well, UVA hasn't made me an offer yet," I said. "It might not happen."

I brought up the practicalities of a move: selling our house, buying a place in Charlottesville, and decluttering our home to make it attractive to buyers. Also, that summer I would attend my last two-week writing residency in July in Vermont.

"We'll have to cancel the trip to the Grand Canyon," Emily said. "Otherwise we won't have enough time to get everything done."

"I think we can do both," I said.

Over nine days, we had planned to tour Bryce, Zion, and the Grand Canyon, meeting up with my sister and her children in Las Vegas, and seeing my mother and two of my brothers in the Bay Area.

Patrick piped in that it would be cool to fly in a plane, while Nicholas and Henrik looked grief-stricken, as if they'd just learned their best friend had died.

"I don't want to hear about this anymore," said Henrik angrily. "You're going to destroy my life if you do this."

Then he stormed down the deck stairs, his head lowered.

"Don't leave angry!" I pleaded, rushing after him. "We can work this out."

He turned around, putting his hand out to stop me from approaching him. "Leave me alone. Don't come near me. You can't take the kids away from me."

My heart ached at his words. We'd established a friendship after years of resentment over a divorce he didn't want. I couldn't hurt him again. We needed to be kind and gentle toward each other as we raised our children. "I haven't gotten the job yet. Maybe I won't. But if I do, I think we can make it work."

Emily, Nicholas, and Patrick stared at their father as he walked on the path toward the asphalt driveway. "Dad, it will be okay," yelled Emily. "I'll be in Virginia so you'll have to go there anyway."

He slammed shut the door of his dark blue Mazda SUV, roared the engine, and drove away.

"I don't blame Dad for being angry," said Nicholas. "I don't want to move either. You're being selfish."

I mechanically stacked the plates, putting the cutlery aside, fighting back tears.

"Let's not talk about it anymore," I said quietly. "I might not get the job anyway."

I reflected on the hours I'd searched for work in journalism. Perhaps I should not have applied to jobs outside New Jersey. No matter how much I yearned for a new job, I had to consider its impact on Henrik. After all, he was the one person nearby whom I could count on.

The next day I sent an email to Tim, thanking him for the interview.

Days crawled by. After work, I immediately checked my phone messages. Several times a day I scanned my email, anxiously looking for Tim's name. A week passed by with no response. My mind changed focus as I reworked questions on school final exams the Wednesday before Memorial Day.

At work, I told Becky about the delay. "It sounds like you didn't get the job," she said. "He'd have contacted you sooner if you had."

All day I tried to discount Becky's remarks, but my mind clouded with doubts. I couldn't take being in limbo, so that afternoon at home, I emailed Tim asking him if he'd decided.

The next day he replied, saying that he'd chosen a man with years of experience at a university, though he was impressed with my credentials. Tears trickled down my face. I sniffled, fleeing to my bathroom for a tissue. I really wanted this job. Wasn't I as capable as the other candidate, even if I'd never worked at a university?

That evening, Nicholas and Henrik rejoiced about the news, though they dampened their enthusiasm out of respect for my feelings. "So you're not going to be close to me," said Emily. "That's sad."

No need to obsess about this disappointment; it would make me depressed. Instead, I imagined happy times ahead through a trip to the Southwest with my family. I thought about how fortunate I was to be able to travel with them.

I called my mom to tell her that I wouldn't be moving from New Jersey anytime soon. "You know, Jenny," she said. "It seemed awfully complicated. You have so much going on this summer. It would have been hard to move. It didn't sound like it was the right time."

No longer did I picture myself working with adults at a university publication. I didn't need to sell my house or look for a new one to buy. The boys could keep their routines, their roots to our little hamlet still intact. That week I avoided Becky, certain she'd point out how she'd been right about the job. Glumly I made copies of French final exams.

Months later, my ex-husband conceded that the move wasn't such a ridiculous idea. "Your identity is tied more to your work than other things," he wisely uttered. "I can understand why you want to return to journalism. But isn't it enough that you're writing for your graduate studies?"

He was right. At a college in Vermont, I was venturing into a literary, long form of writing; my background in journalism helping me craft essays. I had made friends with other writers who also felt the desire to express themselves on blank white pages. I had to stop dwelling on how journalism had once brought me satisfaction. This new phase of my life involved focusing on family and ensuring a financially secure future. I rethought how I viewed my job. It wasn't essential I earn a living through writing. Instead I could do it on the side; that would have to be enough.

The good news was that Harris had rehired me. I was thankful that Laura, who'd been on maternity leave, had decided not to return. She was busy taking care of twin boys, the commute to Harris too long. Instead, that fall she'd be teaching part-time at a job closer to home. Now my future at Harris was more secure. I didn't need to worry about losing a job I was beginning to like. I promised myself to make Harris my second home, aspiring to get tenure so I could stay there indefinitely.

Tenure

Forty-five states have policies for tenure.

Four states have eliminated tenure (FL, KS, NC, WI).

The District of Columbia and North Dakota don't have tenure policies.

Twenty-two states require districts to consider teacher performance.

In most states, tenure is awarded after three years of teaching.

At least ten states require a teacher to return to probationary status because of poor evaluation ratings.

*Source: National Council on Teacher Quality and Education Commission of the States*

## Benefits of Tenure

Ensures teachers cannot be fired without a fair hearing.

Attracts qualified candidates to the profession.

Insulates teachers from favoritism and nepotism.

Allows teachers to stand up to outsiders who instruct them how to teach politically sensitive topics.

Protects teachers from well-connected parents who might push their children's interests.

*Source: American Federation of Teachers*

## Chapter Twenty-Five

# TERRI

In late August, the whole family drove to Virginia to drop off Emily at James Madison University. As we walked around campus, her excitement apparent, I felt slightly resentful. Why couldn't I be starting an adventure in a new place? I squelched the feelings.

Instead I thought about the positives awaiting me that semester: Students were learning French in my school, administrators had praised me for good classroom management, and I'd made friends among faculty. To make my year memorable, I'd build deeper relationships with the people at school. I would embrace the familiar, a place of security where the mind and body felt at ease.

The first days of my second year teaching at Harris School, former students enthusiastically greeted me in the hallways. In class, I relaxed as most students followed my instructions—except one.

Everyone at school knew Terri. What set him apart from other guys was that he dressed as a girl, wearing skin-tight pink shirts, rose-colored lip gloss, and blue eye shadow. His apparel didn't bother me—he was probably gay or transgender—but most students refused to work with him. After a month in class, he had many missing assignments; to prevent him from failing the marking period, I encouraged him to drop by during lunch or after school. I would help him complete the work. One day he took me up on my offer.

At our first meeting, Terri confessed he wanted to be an artist or dancer, maybe even a stripper. Eyeing his black Lycra pants and stiletto heels, I could see him leading a burlesque troupe in a New Orleans carnival. But as a teacher, I couldn't endorse a student, especially someone as smart as Terri, finding work that involved disrobing.

"Why don't you find a job that uses your mind?" I asked. "You're bright."

"Really, you think I'm smart?" he said incredulously.

*Had no one else told him he could succeed at school if he put his mind to it?*

"When you do work, it's very good," I said. "You just need to finish assignments."

I suggested we complete the worksheet on the past tense, which he hadn't handed in, but he wanted to talk about other matters.

"I'm trying out for an MTV show," said Terri, lounging in a student desk. "It would be really cool. It's tough to get a spot."

He explained how thousands of singers and dancers were vying for twenty spots in the national competition. "I know I can do this," he said, stretching out his sturdy legs. "My boyfriend is helping me out."

"It's good you have someone special," I said.

"God, Jake is hot," he said dreamily. "Do you think I'm too fat? I don't want to turn him off. Look at my stomach." He lifted his shirt, grabbing a section of his small belly.

"Everyone has a bit of extra padding," I said. "It's fine."

He'd fit right in with musicians, dancers, and singers, enticing them with his brawny good looks and open, chatty personality. Yet at school, several students had confided in me that it freaked them out that he wore women's clothes. Just before class they whispered about outfits that belonged more in Paris's Red Light district than at a suburban school, no matter the student's gender. Terri had ignored his peers' subtle hints to conform. Students accepted that he was gay, but they didn't want a drag queen in class.

"So when will you know if you're accepted into the program?" I asked.

"A month or two, maybe. I'm not sure."

"Good luck. Next time you come by, let's work on missing assignments. You need to improve your grade."

Our twenty minutes together had passed without any work getting done. Was this something I should have prevented? Should I have insisted he complete the worksheet while I sat beside him, guiding him? He had wanted to talk to me, trusting me enough to reveal his hopes, dreams, aspirations. I was building a connection with a struggling student I liked. The worksheet could wait another day.

I encouraged him to continue working in class with Sarah and seeing me.

"She's pretty much the only friend I have in this place," Terri said.

Wow, that was sad. "We can be friends," I said.

Terri smiled. "I'd like that Madame Nelson."

★ ★ ★

Good ol' Sarah, a Catholic girl originally from Haiti, helped Terri. While sitting next to her, he'd occasionally finish classroom assignments. With her, he often laughed. At least in class, he wasn't thinking about his strained situation at home, and how his father had rejected him. I promised myself that every time I met Terri, I'd remember to follow my alternate route's teacher words of wisdom. "As educators, we must tell students we understand their pain. But we must emphasize that school is a refuge where students should put aside their problems and focus on learning."

Could I convince Terri to see the benefit of learning during class and at our private sessions? As his friend and teacher, I wanted him to pass French, but he would have to cooperate and listen to my suggestions. He ultimately was responsible for his success or failure.

★ ★ ★

Several weeks later, Terri strutted in the classroom wearing snug jeans, a polo shirt, and camel-colored loafers. Where were his high-heeled shoes, pastel tops, and lipstick? "How do you like my new look?" he asked.

"You always look good," I say beaming.

Why had he changed to look like a preppie studying at Harvard? Did he intend to mingle with the school's intellectuals, erasing his status as a loner? I didn't ask him about this transformation; teens cringed at teachers probing into their personal lives. Instead I'd wait for him to bring it up.

As I eyed Terri, I realized I could change my image. I would become the exemplary teacher in Ann Taylor Loft outfits, low-heeled pumps, and practical book bags. I would completely cast off my identity as a stressed, irreverent journalist.

Every month, Terri dropped by to see me. Sometimes we'd get an assignment done together, other times we just talked. He was figuring out who he was and where he was heading. I was happy to provide advice, hoping that I was a bright spot in a place he had admitted hating. I pushed him to complete projects to make it more likely he would pass French. Typically we would start a project together, then he said he'd finish it at home. But I never received the work, despite a few emails reminding him to turn it in. What more could I do to make him see the value of taking school seriously? Perhaps the best I could hope for was to create happy memories for him of laughter and fun in class and in our after-school meetings.

I was feeling more attached to the school, partly due to the fact I was getting closer to students, including Terri. As his friend, I wanted to know if Terri had been accepted into the MTV show, but he never brought it up. I suspected he'd been rejected and didn't want me to know it. Who wants to advertise failure?

I felt proud that I was connecting with Terri despite the difference in our backgrounds. I remembered my mother's words: Your earthly riches might be taken away from you, but what you have stored in your brain will last forever. Educate yourself. Learn as much as you can. Stay curious. I questioned whether Terri had ever gotten that message from his parents. Could I help him understand how earning a high school diploma would help him keep his options open for a job and further studies? Didn't he know that without a degree, it would be difficult to earn a living? I doubted he was thinking so far into the future.

★ ★ ★

One morning before class, he gingerly walked into the classroom and divulged he'd be attending an outpatient clinic to treat depression, bipolar disorder, and schizophrenia. I hadn't seen him manic or depressed; I'd only noticed how he was moody, daydreamed, and drew sketches. Other students sometimes showed the same lack of motivation, so I hadn't thought he was suffering from mental illness.

I was surprised I was just finding out about this. I felt awful that I hadn't picked up on his mental illness. Perhaps he hadn't wanted me to know about it, keeping it secret until professionals determined a set course of action. Wasn't it easier and less embarrassing to pretend one didn't have a condition that impacted one's well-being? I needed to support him as he pursued medical treatment.

"That facility sounds like a great place," I said. "You should get great treatment there."

Certainly the clinic would help him cope with his depression and what could be gender identity issues; his angst might be the result of not knowing if he wanted to be a boy or a girl. He'd go there every day after school and take medication to control his moods. Getting a high school education was very important, but just now Terri had bigger issues to deal with.

The following months Terri's grades plummeted, leading the Child Study Team to flag him for extra intervention from professionals trained to handle students with academic and emotional problems. Betsy Holmes, who had helped me with Anne's issues, summoned Terri and me to a windowless room to talk about strategies that could help Terri pass.

"I'm glad we're meeting again," said Betsy, before Terri arrived to the meeting. "I understand Anne did very well on the final exam in French last year."

"She studied a lot—and it paid off," I said.

"We hope that Terri can have the same outcome," she said.

Terri avoided eye contact, holding his fingers tightly together as if praying for a miracle. "Perhaps Madame Nelson can help me," he said timidly.

*I had been doing that all year. But given his mental state, was this what he should be focusing on?*

Betsy looked over some papers; I wished I could have read what was in his dossier. I wanted to know more about how he was faring at the clinic to treat mental illness. Was he getting any better? Was it now possible for him to concentrate on his studies?

"Terri, your grades have dropped over the year," said Betsy, eyeing her computer screen. "You went from a C and D in the first two quarters, to an F in the third. This isn't what we like to see. Unfortunately, if you don't improve your grade this last marking period, you risk failing French. How did this happen?"

Terri lowered his face.

"It's been difficult for him to complete assignments," I said. "I've been helping him after school. It's tough for him."

What else should I say? Didn't Betsy know he suffered from mental illness? Can schools expect a teenager to complete assignments when he or she has a bipolar disorder and schizophrenia? Or does a young person benefit by working while undergoing treatment for mental conditions? I wasn't qualified to suggest the best course of action. Other professionals in the school oversaw that.

"I didn't know I was doing that bad," said Terri, his eyes tearing up. "The first two marking periods I did good."

That was before he was diagnosed with mental illness; then he had completed some assignments and passed a few quizzes. It was in the spring when he lost focus, spending more time in class drawing captivating images of students' faces, leaving the room to go to the nurse, and seeking extra help from me less frequently.

"Here Terri," I said, handing him a tissue from the box on the table. "We'll see what we can do."

He whisked droplets from his cheeks. I felt like patting him on the back to reassure him we cared.

"To pass French, you need to get a B this marking period," said Betsy. "Would it be possible, Mrs. Nelson, for him to make up some missing assignments?"

"Of course," I said. "Terri, you should come by tomorrow after school."

Betsy ended the meeting by reiterating that Terri should work with me to hand in all assignments and prepare for the final exam.

"Terri, it's up to you to get the work done," said Betsy earnestly. "So many teachers want you to succeed. I spoke with your English teacher, and she admires how you express yourself wonderfully in essays. Please take French class seriously. Mrs. Nelson and I don't want to see you fail. If you get a B this final quarter, you still need a C on the final exam in order to pass for the year."

Terri frowned. "I don't know if I can do that. I don't know French."

"You'll learn by redoing assignments," I said.

He nodded, a slight smile on his face. "I'll try."

Other Harris High School teachers were watching over Terri. In the hallways I heard Vice Principal Connors encouraging Terri. Mrs. Clay, his English teacher, had befriended him, saying he shouldn't let anyone mock him about his sexual identity. I was surprised to find out that the Child Study Team had pinpointed his need for substance abuse treatment. When had that happened? Was he now being treated for alcohol or drug abuse? I hoped he'd drop by soon so I could at least help him pass French.

The following six weeks, Terri changed attitude. He completed his homework, participated in class, and took notes on grammar points. Sarah helped him when he got stuck, he asked me questions when he didn't understand, and he passed quizzes. I congratulated him as his grade rose to a C- for the marking period. It wasn't the B Betsy and I had wanted from him, but if he aced the final exam, he could squeeze by with a 60 percent year-end average.

"I knew you could do it," I told him after class one day. "Learning isn't that complicated. You're very smart—and you worked hard."

"Do you think I can pass the final?"

Well, I explained, he'd need to know the past tense, French speaking countries, proper use of prepositions for places, reflexive verbs to write about daily routine, and monuments in Paris. Could he read a Paris metro map and talk about illnesses and remedies? I recommended he start reviewing the study guide; he had only ten days to master a year's worth of work.

"Is the exam hard?" he asked.

I got tired of students asking me that question, though I always tried to reassure them.

"It's not bad if you know the material. Here's another study guide."

Terri scanned the two-page guide, his eyes downcast. "This is too much to learn. I have no idea what reflexive verbs are."

My class covered that grammar point in the spring when he'd been attending an outpatient client. All year he'd been dealing with sexual identity issues, a critical father who couldn't accept him, and drug abuse. If only he hadn't delayed working until the last marking period after Betsy and I met with him. Would the outcome have been different if intervention had happened earlier?

As a teacher I had to be encouraging, but also honest. I told him he'd need a 75 percent on the final exam to pass the course. The exam was worth ten percent of the grade.

"I'll help you during lunch or after school," I said. "We'll work on a cheat sheet for the final. You can write anything on an 8 ½ by 11 ½ piece of paper and refer to it on the day of the exam. I'm allowing other students to do this."

He didn't stop by my room after school. I would have prepped him for the final, creating the best cheat sheet ever.

In class he assured me he could pass the test; he was writing down French grammar and vocabulary words on a piece of paper. He didn't want to retake French 2. He was such a good artist, I told him, that he should consider becoming a graphic designer. Did he know that the school's vocational training program provided training on that and that the following year, as a junior, he could enroll in it? "That program is for dummies," he said, dismissing the idea.

A week later, Terri arrived at the final exam with no cheat sheet. I didn't have the heart to reprimand him. I wasn't surprised that he failed the French exam, but I dreaded telling him. How could I relate this message without making him seem like a failure?

On the last day of school, I held a mini-conference with my students, showing them their final exam grade and yearly grade point average. In class, I called students up to my desk to go over this information. Terri hesitantly approached me.

"So, did I pass?" he said softly. "I don't think so because I couldn't like answer half the questions. It was an impossible test. I left so many answers blank. I tried to guess for some of them, but I don't know if I got those right either. It was too hard for me."

I shook my head. "No, I'm sorry Terri. You're right—you didn't pass. There was too much material for you to learn in a short period of time. But look at it this way. Next year, French 2 shouldn't be that bad because you'll have learned some of it this year. Easy. You should be able to get an A or B. And you'll be able to speak French. Wouldn't you like that?"

"I just want to be done with high school," he said. "I can't wait to get out of this place."

"You have so much potential," I said. "The last few weeks, you showed me how hard you can work. Next year, just start earlier. All this work will pay off. I'll see you in September."

I wanted to hug him, but the school forbade that. Instead I patted him on the back, wishing him a good summer and telling him I would miss him. In the fall, I assured him he would stay on track from the first day of school to the last.

The following year, Terri took Spanish 1. I was surprised and a little hurt that he had switched languages. After all, I thought we had established a connection and that he would want to learn from me again. I thought about dropping by his Spanish class to ask him how he was doing with his mental illnesses and substance abuse. But that would be viewed as creepy or, worse, stalking a student. If I saw him in the hallway, I would approach him.

Halfway through the year, Terri mysteriously left Harris High

School. Even his friend, Sarah, was clueless of his whereabouts. Perhaps he'd moved to another school district, or he was living at a mental health facility.

The rest of the year as I walked the hallways, I occasionally thought of Terri. I hoped he'd gotten off drugs, addressed his gender identity issues, and perhaps even forgiven his father. Had he found a place where he felt welcomed? At Harris he'd been a loner, but perhaps where he had gone he encountered people like him, who knew how to ease his troubles.

Eighteen months later, his former English teacher mentioned in passing that Terri had moved to Los Angeles. She'd been in contact with him and didn't think he'd finished high school, but she wasn't sure what he was doing in California. Evidently he was still taking drugs. She felt horrible that he might die of a drug overdose, though if he continued with treatment, he should do fine. She didn't know if he had pursued his passion of dancing and drawing. Most importantly, was he happy with whom he had become?

Too much time had passed for me to reach out to him for answers. I hoped he retained good memories of our times together, perhaps taking to heart some of my advice, and remembering me as someone who cared enough to help. Through him, I had learned a key lesson: Recognize that students might be dealing with serious issues. What to do to make their lives easier? Have fun in class. Joke around occasionally. Laugh a little. Listen sympathetically to students. Help them solve their problems. Keep the door wide open for them to enter.

Transgender Youth

A transgender person is someone whose gender identity does not correspond with their sex at birth.

Almost 2% of high school students—at least 1.7 million—identify as transgender.

Trans youth with supportive families experience a 46% decrease in suicide attempts.

Twenty-seven percent of trans youth say their families are very supportive.

Fifty-nine percent of transgender students were required to use a bathroom that did not match the gender they live every day.

Twelve percent of trans youth say their school or district has official policies that support trans students.

*Source: Infographic by the Movement Advancement Project (MAP), Biden Foundation, and Gender Spectrum on the lgbtmap.org website.*

# Chapter Twenty-Six

# A PRIVATE NOTEBOOK

What was it about that morning that brought out the worst in Saniya and Sam, two girls who thus far had never acted up in my class? I was walking around the room, checking students' homework when it all started.

"What the fuck, Sam!" yelled Saniya.

I turned around just in time to see Saniya whack Sam across her delicate cheeks.

"Saniya, what are you doing?" I yelled, rushing to her. "Don't hit her!"

*Is this really happening? What should I do? I'd never broken up a fight before. Should I restrain Saniya, a muscular teen, or protect Sam, a petite girl?*

To shield the blows, Sam covered her face with her hands.

Instinctively I wrapped my arms around Sam's head, creating a barrier between her and the attacker. I felt I was protecting a bunny from a coyote.

Saniya struck again, swiping at the small, exposed top of Sam's head. "Sam, you're a fucking bastard!" screamed Saniya. "And a fucking idiot!"

*Come on. This had to stop. What else could I do? Should I get in between them? Saniya was a lot taller, and at least 20 pounds heavier than me. If she swiped me, I might end up with a concussion.*

Students were appalled by the altercation.

"Oh, my God!" screamed Maddy.

"Saniya, just stop!" yelled Alyssa.

"You're going to get suspended if Dr. Connors finds out," said Andrew.

I was enraged at Saniya's outburst: Normally she was a calm, hardworking girl who never showed animosity. Sam, an outgoing teen, hadn't gotten angry in class; the only thing that made her stand out was that she dyed her hair pink or blue depending on the season.

*I must do something; blows are still coming. Can I move Sam away from the violence?*

"Come on, Sam," I said, tugging on her shirt. "Get up. You need to get away from her."

Sam refused to budge, whimpering, traumatized from the experience.

I glanced around the classroom to see if I could identify a student strong and calm enough to help. Matt fit the bill. "Matt, can you help get Saniya away from Sam?" I said desperately.

"I don't wanna get involved . . ." said Matt calmly. "She might hit me."

I didn't blame Matt for being afraid of Saniya; I was too.

Saniya ignored our pleas to refrain from hitting Sam. Several of Saniya's blows brushed my arm. I felt little pain, but Sam was sobbing, the repeated hits taking a toll on her body.

"I can't take it anymore," said Saniya, bashing Sam. "You're a slut."

I tried to push Saniya away with one arm, but Saniya dodged my hand, backing away from me at the last second.

"Saniya, stop hitting her," I ordered. "Let's talk about what's bothering you."

Several students shut their eyes; they couldn't stomach a classmate being abused. Others commented on how Saniya had serious anger management issues. A few texted on their cell phones, but no one recorded the scene. School rules forbade taking videos in class, though the use of cell phones was left to the teacher's discretion. I allowed my students access to their iPhones for technologically-based activities when they'd left their Chromebooks at home or uncharged.

"You're a real bitch," continued Saniya, venom in her voice. "You can't take someone's private stuff. That was my notebook. Give it back to me."

So this argument was all about a notebook! Whatever Saniya had written on the pages must be so damning that she couldn't handle peers reading it. I imagined a private diary in which she talked about a secret crush on some cute guy, a friendship gone sour due to unkind gossip, or her first experience smoking weed or drinking alcohol. Maybe she penned words about depression or mental anxiety or conflicts with her parents.

Sam groaned as Saniya struck her again. "Please make her stop!" Sam pleaded to me.

It was clear I couldn't resolve this on my own. "Andrew, go get security," I said.

I reassured Sam that a security guard would arrive soon; he would remove Saniya.

After what seemed like ten minutes, but was probably only sixty seconds, Saniya stepped away from Sam.

"She has to give me back my notebook right now," said Saniya. "Where is it?"

"I don't have it," said Sam meekly.

"That's a fucking lie," said Saniya. "I saw you take it from my backpack. Hand it over."

Should I ask Sam to return the notebook? Where was it hidden? In her backpack, locker, or jacket? I didn't have the right to search a student's private property. Later, Dr. Connors would figure out what happened with the notebook.

I understood Saniya's frustration, yet not her violence. As a teen I kept a diary and would have been angry if someone read it without my consent. I grew up before the advent of social media, when gossip was conveyed mainly through conversations. Nowadays, dramatic events could be posted within seconds on Twitter, Instagram, and Facebook. Saniya would be devastated if the whole school knew her secrets, maybe even refusing to come to school. Maybe Sam could partially be blamed for Saniya's outrage, though they could have hashed out their problems in a guidance counselor's office.

Mike, a middle-aged security guard, walked into the room.

"So, which kid should I take?" he asked.

"Saniya Moore," I said, pointing to the tall teen.

Mike walked over to Saniya. "Okay, come with me. You're going to your house office. What was this fight all about?"

I was about to summarize the events, but Saniya beat me to it. "This is fucking ridiculous. I want my notebook back. This is so unfair."

"A notebook isn't worth fighting for," said Mike, grabbing Saniya's arm. "Hey, let's get going. I don't have all day."

Mike led Saniya out of class, shutting the door behind him. Everyone looked relieved. Several students tweeted on their cell phones, and I was sure the incident was circulating to all corners of the building. I pictured Saniya at the office of her grade level administrator getting reprimanded for her inappropriate actions.

Sam looked exhausted, slumped in her chair, her face pink and hair disheveled. Did her body ache after all the blows?

"Sam, you should go to the nurse to make sure everything is okay," I said. "Emily, will you go with her?"

Emily jumped at the chance to help a fellow student—and leave class. She helped Sam out of her chair, holding her arm as they exited. Students immediately rehashed that period's drama: "Can you believe Saniya did that to Sam?" said Alyssa.

"Man, whatever is in that notebook must be freaking nasty," said Maddy.

"You were great, Madame Nelson," said Andrew.

"What an awesome teacher," said Rachel.

I basked in their praise. I'd protected Sam from serious injuries and quickly understood why Saniya had lashed out at Sam. I hadn't freaked out. How different the outcome could have been if I hadn't maintained my cool or not stopped the fight. Or if I'd been at Northern, where students might have reacted differently. I pictured several students egging on the aggressor, while others urged the victim to fight back. Students would have been captivated by the excitement, unwilling to break up the conflict. I would have stood by, paralyzed, uncertain how to control the disaster. I had been lucky no one at Northern had started fights!

"I hope no one knows what was in notebook!" I announced to the class.

Students shook their heads. "No, we have no idea," said Maddy.

Thank goodness, the contents of Saniya's journal remained private to at least the students in this class.

★ ★ ★

After class, I talked to Dr. Connors about the incident. She recommended I separate Sam and Saniya, sitting them on opposite sides of the classroom. They must never work together on assignments. She praised me for how I handled the situation. As an administrator, she had broken up many conflicts, mainly in the cafeteria where students socialized more. The scenario often involved one student impulsively saying something nasty, another taking it personally, and before long, the incident escalated into pushing or shoving. That was why so many staff members were assigned cafeteria duty; that was where most fights occurred. So I mustn't take it too seriously, she said, since it was a normal part of the job.

Later I discovered how many other teachers had fights in their classrooms. "It really has nothing to do with you," said a history teacher. "It sometimes happens, unfortunately."

I was glad my school took rules seriously. Saniya would get an out-of-school suspension, and Sam, a Saturday detention for taking the notebook. Administrators would notify parents of their children's misbehavior and the need to discipline them. I hoped there would not be another fight in my classroom; but if there was, I'd know what to do.

# The Prevalence of Crime at Schools

Three quarters of public schools experienced one or more incidents of crime in the 2019-2020 academic year. This amounted to 1.4 million incidents.

That year, 70% reported violent incidents such as physical attacks and fights without a weapon, and threats of physical attack without a weapon.

One quarter of schools recorded serious violent incidents, such as rape or attempted rape; and fights, physical attacks and robbery with a weapon.

Almost one-third of schools reported incidents of theft.

*Source: National Center for Education Statistics*

## School Shootings

In 2022, 51 school shootings resulted in injuries or deaths.

That year, 39 people were killed and 101 injured, the highest number of casualties in the past five years.

Twenty-one of the deaths occurred at Robb Elementary School in Uvalde, Texas.

Thirteen school shootings happened at sporting events.

*Source: Education Week*

## Chapter Twenty-Seven

# WHO IS THE PROFESSIONAL?

The following September, I was thrilled Harris High School agreed to hire me part-time; I would earn money in the morning by teaching and satisfy my creative desires by writing in the afternoons for my graduate studies in creative writing. Enrollment in French had surged, partly due to my success at convincing students French was more exciting than Spanish or German. To meet the demand of thirteen sections of French—instead of its usual ten or eleven—the school hired another full-time French teacher, Vail.

Becky, the veteran French teacher, described Vail as a chatty, middle-aged hippie. With eight years teaching experience, she never earned tenure at previous schools. This tidbit of information worried me. Maybe she hadn't stayed three years in a district because she'd been an incompetent teacher. Perhaps she had been fired due to poor evaluations. During professional development days, I would find out. I hoped we would get along well enough to successfully share a room with my using the classroom in the mornings and her in the afternoons; otherwise, it would be a long year.

I entered my classroom and looked up to see a gray-haired woman standing on a step ladder taping up posters. In navy blue capris and white sandals, she looked more like an aging sailor than a hippie. "How do you like where I put the posters?" said Vail, smiling sweetly.

*Why hadn't she deferred to me, a veteran teacher, to decorate the room?*

"Some posters might not work where they are," I said, eying the walls. "Why don't we move the Renoir to the front?"

The poster's café scene brought back memories of good times in France; I wanted it center stage. As we took it down, Vail suggested we occasionally go out for coffee to recharge during what would be a demanding year. I didn't envy her being a new teacher, but with my advice, maybe she wouldn't struggle as much as I had at Northern.

"Do you understand the rotating schedule?" I said, showing her a calendar with A, B, C and D days.

"It's still confusing," she said, worriedly.

"It looked complicated my first year at school," I said. "Then it clicked. I'll show you what makes it easy."

I opened up my planner with its kaleidoscope of color-coded French classes. She looked perplexed as I pointed out which classes I taught on which days. "I have to be back at new teacher orientation soon," she said impatiently. "Let's just finish the posters."

"I can tell you which students to watch out for," I said, eying her roster of students.

"I prefer to discover students on my own," she said.

*Wow, I was just trying to make her life easier. Evidently she pre-ferred decorating instead of preparing for teaching's practicalities. Her priorities weren't straight.*

"You know today is my birthday," she said. "Are you available for a drink later?"

"No, I have to make dinner for my kids," I said. "By the way, if you don't mind my asking, how old are you?"

"Sixty-one," she said proudly.

I would have guessed she was in her fifties. She was nearing retirement; why hadn't she yet found a district to call home?

★ ★ ★

Several weeks later, I learned more about Vail's shortcomings when I asked her if we could swap classrooms third period. I was tired of lugging materials between classrooms, and since she had study hall that period, it would be an easy switch.

"If it will help you out, I'll do it," she said primly. "But I'm not happy about it. My study hall has some challenging students. Besides, you know how anal Becky is about her room."

Becky was a neat freak, requiring every item be stored in a certain place, and returned to its original location, no exceptions. After each class I scurried, picking up papers and putting textbooks back on shelves. The times I left something behind, Becky had made it known.

I emailed Dr. Connors requesting the change; the next day, she approved it. By then Vail had reconsidered. "It's too much for me," she said. "I don't have a handle on my study hall."

*Really! Was she appealing the administration's decision?*

"Vail, I leave worksheets behind in our classroom, and then I have to teach without them," I pleaded. "Does it really matter where study hall is?"

"I can't help you," she said, adamantly.

*What a pain in the butt. Why this change of heart? Had someone convinced her she could stay in our classroom because she was full-time and I, part-time?*

"I have strategies for students who act up in study hall," I said, seething. "Find out what classes a student is failing. Then tell him he must work in study hall to bring up that grade."

"That's a bad idea," said Vail. "This group is awful. They don't care about academics."

I was dumbfounded. Was she delusional in believing her

study hall students would behave worse in a different classroom?

"You'll have to tell Dr. Connors why you can't switch study hall," I said. "She won't like how you changed your mind."

Out of empathy for a new teacher, I helped Vail pen an email to Dr. Connors. Maybe I felt compassion for a newcomer, struggling to control teenagers. Vail could also misrepresent the situation, making me appear unprofessional.

Later that morning I ran into Dr. Connors in the hallway. She had gotten Vail's email but decided I should teach in the room where my materials were. Vail would be assigned another classroom. Hallelujah! I thanked her for supporting me but mentioned that Vail would be livid.

"Vail will be fine," she said. "It's tough the first month, but she'll adjust."

Vail reluctantly moved her study hall students to Becky's room, sullen she hadn't gotten her way. I imagined Vail dreaded seeing those students, no matter what room she was in. Why hadn't she taken my advice about strategies to quiet them down? She seemed like a know-it-all, and that became ever clearer as time went on.

The following Tuesday, as I prepared to leave our classroom, one of Vail's students approached me. "Do you know which teachers are absent today?"

"Let me check," I said, logging on to the computer to retrieve the list of absent teachers. "Here's the absentee list. I'll print it out."

As I pressed the printer button, the bell rang and Vail walked into the classroom.

*I must leave the room immediately. Vail will be angry if I don't. I know the rule. When sharing a room, a teacher must vacate it when the other teacher arrives.*

The printer light blinked red. Had Vail again forgotten to

replenish paper or jammed it by pushing random buttons?

I opened the printer's door; yes, no paper. Students trickled in, noisily retrieving folders. I loaded paper, and finally, the absentee list printed out. Vail approached me.

"Madame Nelson, *il faut que tu partes maintenant, la cloche a sonné. C'est ma salle de classe*," she yelled. *Mrs. Nelson you must leave now. The bell rang. It's my classroom.*

Students ceased chattering. I wanted to tell her I had stayed to help a student, but her tone of voice made it clear she would not accept an explanation. Without hesitation I dashed out of the room, handing Akim the absentee list as I passed him. My heart beat twice as fast as normal. I overheard students murmuring: "Did she really yell at Madame Nelson?" "I can't believe Mrs. Lackey did that."

The hallway's desolation didn't soothe me. I had to tell someone about my mistreatment. I headed to the world language workroom, my mind swirling with anger, sadness, and confusion. No teacher had ever screamed at me, much less in front of students. Why was she threatened by my staying behind? Was she also struggling to discipline this group of teens?

Turning the corner to the science wing, I spotted Dr. Connors. "Are you okay?" she asked.

Was it that obvious I was upset? "Yes, I'm fine."

"You seem out of sorts," said Dr. Connors. "Is everything okay between you and Vail?"

I paused; I didn't want to badmouth Vail nor lie to Dr. Connors. "Vail yelled at me to leave the room," I said hesitantly. "I was helping a student. It only took a minute or two."

"What did she say exactly?"

"She told me in French that I had to leave immediately," I said. "It was her classroom; I shouldn't be there."

Dr. Connors laughed. "That's funny. It's anxiety from the start of school. It's just nerves."

Really? Nerves? She was nasty and unprofessional; Dr. Connors should not dismiss it so quickly. "A teacher has never yelled at me."

"Don't take it personally. Vail didn't mean it. Remember how it was being new? I'll talk to her. Just let it go."

How long ago it seemed when Dr. Connors had guided me to ensure I succeeded. I'd forgive Vail, but she had to apologize.

The next morning I anxiously walked into Room 121, twenty minutes before class began. Vail was typing at the computer, papers scattered everywhere. "How dare you go behind my back and tell Dr. Connors what goes on in my classroom!" she fumed. "She's my supervisor, the one who evaluates me. No one has ever done that to me before."

*So much for the apology.*

I tried to interrupt her. She ranted on about how I was unprofessional and uncaring; colleagues were supposed to support each other, not rat on them. Finally she stopped when several students entered the room. Only fifteen minutes until the period started.

"I ran into Dr. Connors in the hallway," I interjected quietly. "She asked me what was wrong."

"So you went to Dr. Connors!" she said, her face flaming red. "That's no way to react to a situation. Go tell the vice principal!"

*What a temper! She mustn't scream at me again in front of students.*

"Vail, it wasn't like that," I said.

"I want to talk to Becky," she said. "Let's see what she says about this."

"We can resolve this on our own," I said.

"I don't think so. You're out to get me."

*Really? She sees me as the enemy! What about the advice I'm giving her?*

She stomped out of the room; I reluctantly followed. In the room next door, Becky was grading at her desk. "Jennifer told Dr. Connors about what happened in class yesterday," she blurted out. "How could she do that to a colleague?"

*Would she ever let me speak? Was this how she acted with her students: never allowing their voices to be heard?*

Vail continued her monologue. Becky and I stood by, silently.

"She's awful. I'm working so hard in this place, getting to know kids, setting up the room. Whatever! I don't know if I can teach here anymore."

*I had to defend myself. This was getting out of hand.*

"Vail, let me talk! You were the one yelling at me in class," I said. "I stayed to help one of your students. I was printing out a list of absent teachers for him."

"I don't care what you have to say," she said seething. "How could you go to my supervisor? You're telling her nasty things about me. What's wrong with you?"

Becky looked astonished at the unfolding drama. "Calm down. We don't need to yell."

Vail continued her accusations, ignoring Becky's attempts to reason with her. Finally Becky walked to the door to lock it. Students couldn't witness this confrontation.

Becky and I stood by as Vail vented. I glanced at the clock: only five minutes until Becky and I taught.

"I'm going to talk to Dr. Connors now and resign," she said. "I can't work with someone who goes behind my back and talks to my supervisor."

*That's a brilliant idea! I don't want her around. She's not good for students or staff. We will be better off without her.*

She moved toward the door; Becky blocked her way. "Please don't do that," she said. "You need to think about this. You're too emotional to make a decision."

"It's almost 7:30," I said. "I teach in a few minutes."

So did Becky, but she didn't seem to care.

"Let's talk later," said Becky. "Vail, you should reconsider quitting. We need you here."

I walked silently toward the door. She and Becky were allies. I didn't dare mention that if Vail left, we would be fine. I would teach three more classes, and Becky one; that would leave one section to fill, and those students could be divvied up among existing classes. Go Vail and resign immediately. Good riddance!

"*Au revoir*," I said to no response.

★ ★ ★

That night I woke up at 2 a.m., my mind whirling over the previous day's event. I couldn't take Vail screaming at me, messing up the printer, and stealing my French materials. I too felt like quitting. A nearby district needed a middle school French teacher; I could send them my resume. But I was used to Harris and had no problems with students; that wasn't guaranteed elsewhere. Besides, if I left, who would lead the trip to France in April?

The next morning as I drove to work, my cell phone rang. It was Vail. I hesitated to pick it up. I didn't want to talk to her, but maybe she had resigned. "Hello," I said hesitantly.

"Jennifer, I'm sorry about what I said yesterday. I hope this doesn't impact our ability to work together."

Was she nuts? Of course, it would, but she had apologized, so I should forgive her. "Sure," I said curtly.

"I woke up at four thinking about you," she said. "Let's try to work together."

*I could manage without her, but would she succeed without my help?*

"Fine, Vail," I said. "I need to focus on driving."

I put my phone in my purse. Why had she reconsidered quitting? I pictured her speaking to her husband about retirement in their lavish home at the shore. She wanted to move to Florida to lower their costs and leave behind cold winters. But he was happy where he was. Perhaps he had urged her to continue working so that she'd qualify for a state pension. With the additional income, they might be able to afford to remain put.

That morning I didn't see Vail wheeling her bag in the hall, looking as if she were about to board a flight to Bermuda. Her Ann Taylor Loft sweater wasn't draped around our shared black vinyl chair. Much to my relief, she avoided me. I left our classroom as soon as the bell rang. That day Becky didn't speak to me, either. We were managing on our own, letting time mitigate the tensions and animosity between us.

Eventually I found out Vail hadn't gotten tenure at her former school because of a student's complaint about her teaching. That same girl later hit a vice principal, but by then, Vail's career had been damaged. The following year she evidently left school to stay at home to grieve the loss of her brother. I believed she hadn't been able to find another teaching job. Now, Harris had become her chance to show she could teach.

Over the course of the next few weeks, Vail's students confided in me: They didn't like Madame Lackey, her class was boring, they weren't learning anything. They missed their old French 1 class with me. Couldn't I teach them French 2? I gave them a blanket response: Madame Lackey had a different teaching style, she was adjusting to a new school, be kind to her, and do the work.

With time, as Vail showed me kindness, I commiserated with her. It was awful how a student commented on Vail's sagging breasts. I agreed it wasn't Vail's fault a girl stuck her finger in a wall outlet, requiring the nurse to remove it with Vaseline.

After falling twice in class, Vail started limping. What had she tripped on? A janitor could remove those objects. She had gained ten pounds after gorging on chocolate to reduce the stress of teaching. I promised to bring in low-calorie apples and carrot sticks for her to munch on.

I felt sorry for Vail. She was burned out. I worried she wouldn't make it to June.

By Thanksgiving, parents were complaining about Vail: She took weeks to put in grades; gave students participation points based on behavior, not achievement; and taught using only worksheets. After Christmas break, administrators criticized her for unstructured lessons that randomly switched topics. They requested I help her write coherent lesson plans and follow my teaching practices. By then it was too late. She admitted she hated her French 1 period 6 class; nor were her other classes going much better.

In April, students were spreading rumors that Vail wouldn't return in September. Her year had thus far been a disaster. Should I tell administrators I could take over her French 1 class? At Northern, Nabila had saved me from weeks of misery by stepping in to teach my Dirty Dozen.

In May, Vail announced she was retiring; students believed she was fired. She said she couldn't take another year like the one she'd just endured. She qualified for a pension by buying back a year of service, and to save money, she mentioned selling her shore house and moving to a condo in Florida. I was relieved she wouldn't come back to Harris that fall. I told Dr. Connors I'd like to teach full time so the district wouldn't need to hire another teacher. Also, I felt confident I could balance teaching during the day with writing evenings and weekends.

The last day of school of my third year teaching at Harris High School, Vail and I straightened up the classroom together, removing posters, organizing filing cabinets, and stacking textbooks. Vail talked about how she was looking forward to a relaxing summer at the beach with visits from her grown children. The room gradually returned to its clean, tidy state.

I reflected on how I had transformed into a veteran teacher who advised first-year teachers. It had been a long journey to feel at ease in a classroom of teens. I felt proud about learning lessons on surviving and thriving teaching high school. Papers still needed to be thrown away, the cabinets cleared of clutter, but I told Vail I'd do that after I spoke to Dr. Connors about my final evaluation and teaching six sections of French—instead of the normal five—so there wouldn't be a need to employ a third French teacher.

When I returned to the classroom, Vail had left. I never officially said goodbye to her. I was disappointed. I wanted to congratulate her on making it through a tough year, wishing her the best in retirement. On the desk she'd left a note. "Thanks for all your help this year, Jennifer. It's been a pleasure working with such a professional. Good luck next year. I'll miss you."

# What to Do if You're a Bored Teacher

Remember what once made you excited to teach. Recreate that feeling. Students haven't yet heard your great lesson. Pretend this isn't the zillionth time you've taught it.

Share your passions with students. Remember students recall how you made them feel.

Humor is good. Show you care. Make students laugh. You will lighten up too. You'll feel energized from their enjoyment.

Participate in projects. Help students create a project using materials from home. You will have fun as students see a different side of you.

Tweak lessons to make them more interesting. Add an element of surprise to them. Discover new things about the material.

Seek advice from colleagues about reigniting your spark. They will share ideas about bringing back enthusiasm. In the process, a colleague could become a friend.

Let students teach a lesson one day. You can take a seat in the audience. It's time they show you what they've learned.

## Chapter Twenty-Eight

# TRIP TO FRANCE

April of the following year, with misgivings, I traveled to France with twenty-five students, three chaperones, and two parents. The school year had passed quickly with my teaching six sections of French, helping with the French Club and Honor Society, and planning a trip to France. That spring, just before Easter break, everything was in order: bags packed, medical forms completed, and plane tickets and hotel reservations confirmed. Students were excited about finally visiting the foreign country they'd studied for years. I fretted I'd be blamed if a student got into serious trouble. Not in a million years could I foresee a chaperone would come the closest to marring the trip.

In a final meeting, the principal gave us his blessing, emphasizing he was confident everyone would follow Harris High School's rules. This meant no drinking, drugs, fighting, or wandering off unescorted. Any misbehavior would be handled swiftly with the student flying home at the parents' expense. I knew most students would take the principal's words seriously; I feared that only Aliya, a high-spirited teenager who loved *Les Misérables*, would think about disobeying us.

I imagined Aliya sneaking out at night and getting drunk at a brasserie on the Champs-Elysées. Or she would stray while touring the Louvre, befriending a French guy and disappearing for hours. I pictured her smoking pot in her hotel room, belting out the lyrics to "In my Life," and coming to dinner high—or not at all. Yet before the trip, Aliya and her mother assured me she would behave; I had to trust her.

One of the chaperones promised to watch over Aliya. After raising four children, my brother Jeff understood how teenagers played pranks and got into trouble. Like Aliya, he was an artist, so could relate to her. Perfect. No need to worry.

On our first night in Paris, after a long day travelling and touring, Jeff berated me for being the world's worst manager. In our hotel room, he complained I was bossing him around like an employee.

"You tell me what to do, and I have to do it," he said, sipping a glass of wine. "I have to spend all day schlepping around teenagers. This is the worst."

No wonder Jeff decided decades ago never to become a teacher. On the verge of finishing his teaching degree, he realized he couldn't handle adolescents. How would he manage ten days with us? Had I made a huge mistake in bringing him along?

"You know you can't do this without me," Jeff said. "I'm great with kids. They love me. They don't seem to like you."

*What the heck! He just said he resented spending time with them.*

"We'll be fine without you," I said, calmly. "You don't have to be a chaperone. You could fly home early."

"Is that the way you solve the problem?" demanded Jeff. "Just get rid of the person by putting him on the next flight to Newark? You need to learn how to manage adults."

How ironic I was accused of ineffectively leading adults, when for years I floundered controlling teenagers. I wouldn't let Jeff impact how I felt about the trip. It wasn't possible for him to fly home early, so to get along, I would ignore him. I left him to his own devices, relieving him of his duties as a chaperone. With time he might resume his responsibilities, but if not, I could depend on other chaperones, as well as Thierry, our French group leader.

In Paris, I watched Grant and his buddies race up the Eiffel Tower, one of them earning the distinction of our group's fastest runner. Matt loved the caricature that a Montmartre artist drew of him, highlighting his enormous eyes and wavy hair, topped with a red beret; he'd give it to his girlfriend back home, promising they would someday return to Paris together.

At the Louvre, I rescued Manav's group from sitting outside a gift shop near the museum's entrance, unable to reenter without a group pass I obtained from a hidden administrative office. At the Centre Pompidou, street performers entertained us with French skits that my students were able to comprehend. Every day brought a minor medical issue, though each was easily resolved by accessing a chaperone's First Aid kit or visiting a nearby pharmacy.

On our last day in Paris, students cheered as I jumped the turnstile in the metro after my ticket malfunctioned, the closing gates snagging my bag overloaded with students' medical documents. Many laughed at my criminal deed, a few recording it on their cell phones. So much for Madame religiously following rules! The tension I'd felt about the trip disappeared; I learned I could trust my students.

I was no longer annoyed at Jeff, who was connecting with teenagers. He explained to Matt how gypsies swindled tourists at the Eiffel Tower in a betting game with moving cups and a coin. I appreciated how Jeff herded students on tours of Paris and watched over Aliya, whose bossiness was turning off students.

Provence brought its own special memories, some bitter, others endearing. With the help of chaperones, I kept everyone safe and was able to handle crises, including news from back home of the death of a Harris High School student.

At the gardens at the Palais des Papes, students scampered up eight-foot boulders overlooking the Rhone River, standing straight up, waving their arms. Aliya precariously balanced on platform sandals, while Grant appeared more stable in sensible sneakers. There was no metal railing on top of the rocks to prevent a person from tumbling down the ravine.

"Hey guys, get down from there," I yelled, my heart racing. "You're making me nervous."

"We're good, Madame Nelson," said Grant with confidence. "We know what we're doing."

*Didn't he realize I couldn't take risks with students? Parents expected me to keep their children safe all the time.*

"*On y va,*" I said, gesturing them to leave. "This is too scary."

The kids jumped down, moaning that climbing was fun and not dangerous. I disagreed, picturing Mademoiselle Platform Shoes slipping and tumbling to her death in the river below.

"Thanks for following directions," I said, my heart rate slowing. "You guys are great."

Then Grant and Aliya raced ahead on the dirt path to our next meet-up location; I cautiously descended the hill. At the bottom, on a stone terrace bench, I spotted Christina, a usually cheerful student, sobbing uncontrollably. Mehta, whom I dubbed our surrogate mother, rubbed Christina's back. As I approached, I heard Mehta say it was okay to let out grief.

The news was all over Facebook: Richard Garcia, a senior at Harris, had died in a crash in his all-terrain vehicle. He had been a daredevil, recklessly driving his ATV over hills and vacant lots.

I imagined Harris High School students paralyzed by the shock of losing one of their own. Behind closed doors, counselors met privately with teenagers, while the principal gathered everyone in the auditorium to memorialize the life of someone far too young to die. In France, I didn't have access to these professionals.

What could adults in my group do to ease students' pain? I summoned the chaperones, parent travelers, and French group leader, Thierry. I urged everyone to be extra sensitive about students' feelings, listening and sympathizing with their loss. We needed to pay particular attention to those close to Richard. Mehta had already consoled Christina. Had other students been friends with Richard? Would this soothe the pain for those in the throes of reconciling life without a person they loved? I wasn't sure, but this was all I knew how to do.

That day I comforted Aliya as she cried over Richard, her best friend. I advised Christina and her to exchange stories about good times with Richard, forever preserving his memory in their minds. I told her they could always share their feelings with me and other adults in our group.

I didn't have the heart to reprimand Aliya for an array of subsequent misdeeds. She criticized Thierry for not talking about Victor Hugo and *Les Misérables*—a repeat of her conversations in class months earlier. She called Ali a loser after he refused to climb the Roman temple in Nimes, nervous he'd fall. In addition, Aliya forfeited her bra to boys during a game of Truth and Dare. And after a chaperone had reprimanded her for that, Aliya called her a bitch. Later, Jeff told her the world didn't revolve around her.

Though she was alienating others, Aliya still hadn't done anything so egregious that warranted sending her home.

★ ★ ★

During our last days in Provence, I began to see students as members of my family. At a restaurant in Nice, we celebrated Grant's fifteenth birthday with a cake from a local patisserie. As we belted out "Happy Birthday," I realized that a closeness had developed: the students had begun to feel like temporary sons and daughters. I had guided and advised them—as any good mother would do—and ensured they'd had fun in a country far from home. Even Aliya, the black sheep, had followed many of the rules. Although the students could never replace my own three kids, for ten days I was becoming closer to them.

At the song's end, Grant blew out the candles. I helped pass out slices of cake, and when I came to Shreya, she beamed. "Jenny Patel, this has been the greatest trip," she said. "It changed my life. You're the coolest person ever."

I'd earned this nickname because I resembled the mother in an Indian soap opera. I was the mom, and Shreya, the glamorous young woman. On this trip, I had become their substitute and devoted mom. What would my former students at Northern think about how much I had changed? Honestly, if I could go back there, I believe I would impress them, showing them generosity and warmth—and comfort and ease in working with all sorts of young people.

At our last dinner in Nice, during dessert, the kids started wildly waving their hands and giggling. What was that all about? It took me a few seconds to figure out they were mimicking me; evidently, I had an endearing method of moving my hands while conversing in French with our guide Thierry. They were teasing me. I joined in the laughter. In Provence, Madame Nelson had become fun-loving, less serious and stressed.

For too long in the classroom, I had buried this animated side of my personality, nervous students wouldn't take me seriously. I reserved light-heartedness for private functions with family and friends. This didn't need to be the case. I would bring back to class this new me, one unafraid of showing students a spectrum of emotions. Finally I was relaxed enough to be myself around teenagers; never again would I doubt my ability to teach well.

Benefits of
Student Travel

Enhances classroom instruction.

Brings subject matter to life.

Promotes cultural understanding.

Broadens students' horizons.

Increases motivation.

Encourages independence.

Boosts self-confidence.

Allows discovery of new interests.

## Chapter Twenty-Nine

# POST PANDEMIC

I t was a chilly October afternoon. Glancing out the windows at
the school's entrance, I caught a glimpse of golden-brown
leaves drifting from summer roosts on the neighborhood oaks as I
rushed to a pivotal faculty meeting. A pandemic had changed education and the world. I entered my school's dimly lit auditorium
for the after-school October faculty meeting, one of the first in-
person encounters since Covid-19 had closed schools two years
before. Other teachers shuffled in, sitting down in comfortable,
red velvet seats. Some texted on cell phones, while others chatted
with colleagues or shut their eyes to get a few moments rest. I
plopped down next to my good friends Maria and Luisa.

"Do you know what's on the agenda today?" I asked Maria, a
middle-aged Spanish teacher.

"Something about data," she answered.

"It can't be about SGOs," I said. "We just did that."

Each year, district administrators required teachers to use
data to guide their teaching. They encouraged analyzing students'
scores from district, state, and national tests to gauge students'
strengths and weaknesses in reading, writing, math, and science. I
had mastered pulling data, posted internally on the district's
website, to prepare my SGO (Student Growth Objective), an annual test to evaluate student learning in every course.

"These SGOs are so ridiculous," added Luisa, a no-nonsense

seventy-year-old German teacher. "They're a waste of time. You just get them done, and that's that. No one really looks at them."

It was best to keep Luisa from being negative on requirements we couldn't change.

"They're due next week, right?" I asked.

"I worked on mine over the weekend," said Maria. "I'm sure Terrillo will email us to tell us to turn them in the next day. I want to be prepared."

Trust Maria, with seventeen years teaching in the district, to be on top of her professional responsibilities. Every morning at 7:15 when I greeted her in her classroom, she was busy finalizing lessons, entering grades in the computer, and refilling pencil jars. As it was for me, teaching was her second career; she'd spent a decade as a flight attendant.

"With the SGOs, we know how to make ourselves and the kids look good," I said. "Have you finished yours, Luisa?"

Luisa shook her head. "Not yet."

"Terrillo is so overwhelmed with supervising several departments that he's not going to be fussy with SGOs," I said.

Ron Terrillo was temporarily supervising the world language, business, and fine arts departments until the district found a permanent hire. He admitted that as a former music teacher and current vice principal, he wasn't an expert on foreign language acquisition and instruction. We foreign language teachers assured him we knew what we were doing—and didn't need much oversight. We were used to new, inexperienced bosses. Over seven years we had five supervisors, the last one resigning in June.

That fall of 2022, my district, as well as others nationwide, was dealing with an acute teacher shortage. Not enough young people—mainly millennials born from 1981 to 1996—were entering the profession; instead drawn to jobs with higher wages and fewer hours. Lack of respect and support for teachers, debates about classroom control, and changing curriculum also contributed to the problem. Teachers were burned out after years of conducting lessons online during the pandemic, then easing into hybrid learning, and finally returning to in-person instruction. I wasn't the only teacher who found many Gen Z students—born from 1997 to 2012—undisciplined and misbehaved. Some teachers also suffered from what's known as "decision fatigue." Research has shown that educators make more minute-by-minute decisions than brain surgeons.

As I looked around the auditorium, I saw exhausted faculty members—and this was only five weeks into the academic year. What would we be like in June? No wonder almost two in five teachers were planning to quit in the following two years, according to a June 2022 survey of members of the American Federation of Teachers, the nation's second largest teachers' union. Was I going to be one of them?

Maria still looked perky, her curly locks framing her exuberant face, a long gray sweater and gold and blue scarf gracing her body. Luisa, the school's sole German teacher, resumed reading a book on the Habsburg monarchy, unperturbed by the profession's demands. She had taught way too long—about four decades—to ever feel anxious.

I glanced at my watch. The meeting would start in two minutes with remarks by the principal, then a presentation by Mandy DePaul, the assistant superintendent of curriculum and assessment. By attending the mandatory meeting, teachers received an hour of professional development—ten of which were required by the district and twenty by the state.

As he approached the podium, Principal Tyson Winzer greeted staff and faculty.

"You're doing a great job in the classrooms to make students feel welcomed," said Winzer, a fifty-four year old with a protruding stomach, graying hair, and infectious smile. "We count on you to help kids adjust to in-person learning after years at home. It's been tough for us as administrators dealing with students, some of whom have not stepped into a school building for two and a half years. We are serious about having to discipline students."

More students were receiving after school and Saturday detentions and in-school and out-of-school suspensions for violating school rules. Administrators were cracking down on dress code abuses—no cropped tops, mini-skirts, and spaghetti straps—and discouraging cell phone use and instead using their Chromebooks for technology-based lessons. The school was also considering reinstating bells.

"We're going back to what it was like in 2019 before the pandemic," said Winzer, pacing in front of the stage.

"So maybe this means we're going to have final exams in June," I whispered to Maria.

"Who knows?" she said, shrugging her shoulders.

"We should fail students who don't learn anything," I said.

"I agree," she muttered.

For too long, administrators had strongly encouraged teachers to pass students at all costs even when they'd done little work and even less mastering of a topic. Academic rigor and scholarly achievements slipped during the pandemic.

Assistant Superintendent Mandy thanked the principal, then on a giant screen she projected graphs showing how standardized test scores had plummeted dramatically in the last three years. Students from elementary school to ninth grade were not proficient in reading and math, according to statewide data. They weren't prepared for the demands of college nor the workplace.

The district's students performed much worse than the state's average.

"Is this a big surprise to you?" she asked the teachers in the auditorium. "It was to me."

No one blurted out their feelings about the grim statistics. I, for one, wasn't shocked given how administrators had encouraged leniency in grading. The first year of remote learning, they had lowered standards necessary to pass a class, making it almost impossible for students to fail. Teachers were advised to limit the number of assignments, grade based on a pass/no pass system, and count only a certain percentage of the student's work. This resulted in inflated grades in June 2020. I had never given so many As to students who did so little work.

The following 2020-2021 academic year wasn't much better. Administrators cancelled final exams, evidently believing these tests would stress students. We were to take it easy on students, watering down curriculum and standards. Many teenagers were suffering from mental illness after being socially isolated during lockdown; the district didn't want them to feel more anxious by reinstating a robust academic program. Perhaps the district worried about lawsuits from parents, who could argue their children hadn't received the education they had been promised, so it was unfair to evaluate them based on previous standards. Grades mattered immensely to parents and students, though I began to question what it meant to get an A in French when the student could barely communicate in the language.

Earlier that month, a nationwide test known as the National Assessment of Education Progress or the Nation's Report Card recorded plunging math and reading levels for fourth and eighth graders. The tests showed the largest ever drop in math scores and a decline in reading that wiped out three decades of gains.

The US Department of Education said scores were a reminder of the pandemic's impact on learners and urged districts to beef up recovery efforts including tutoring.

Now districts across the nation were playing catch up. It wasn't going to be easy to change the tide. Students were now accustomed to slacking off during remote learning. Without teachers and peers in the same room, their behavior had deteriorated. I surmised parents had left teenagers to their own devices; confident they had learned since their grades were good. During the pandemic, motivated students—those who aimed to go to highly selective colleges—had taken school seriously, learning enough to seamlessly make the transition from high school to college. I wasn't as confident about the less ambitious students, who struggled to complete assignments during remote learning.

For almost eight months—from mid-March 2020 to mid-January 2021—students in my district learned at home. Several mornings a week, I'd meet them on Google Meet to give instruction. Many would be propped up in bed, their room darkened, stuffed animals near their side. At my urging they'd turn on their video cameras, but once I started teaching, many screens went blank. They argued they couldn't hear me with the video on. Nor would they answer my questions, some saying their microphone didn't work properly. After months of talking to the void I grew discouraged, eventually giving up on creating a dialogue with them.

Instead, after a three- to five-minute lesson on vocabulary, grammar, or culture, I posted assignments. They had two to three days to turn in the work, much longer than what I'd required pre-pandemic. Administrators didn't want me to assign work that was too taxing. I followed orders.

That year, with the help of my techno savvy millennial son, I mastered educational technology platforms including EdPuzzle,

Quizlet, NearPod, Robotel's SmartClass Media, and the online textbook. At first I didn't believe I could create lessons online, but that year proved me wrong. I taught without the use of a hard copy textbook, workbook, paper handouts, and white eraser board. I felt a little like a Gen Z.

Fortunately, years earlier, my district had provided Chromebooks to students and staff, so we were accustomed to Google Classroom and other online educational tools. Administrators made sure every student was connected to the Internet—no matter where they lived. This wasn't the case in other parts of our country, particularly rural areas where Internet was non-existent, or signals weak.

Virtually, students made PowerPoint Presentations on topics that included French amusement parks, vacations in Paris, and French speaking countries and presented them during class time on Google Meet. They also recorded videos on FlipGrid on global social issues such as poverty, homelessness, climate change, and education. Students took notes on a Google Doc about what they had learned. We were managing in this new reality, even though technology sometimes proved cumbersome, and I longed for the simplicity of asking students to fill out a worksheet.

Those pandemic days seemed distant as Mandy finished her presentation on the dismal performance of our students in reading and math. She dismissed us from the auditorium to the cafeteria, telling us to discuss how to improve student performance and write suggestions on Post-it notes and tape them on posters in the room. Around a lunchroom table, my colleagues and I talked about ways to improve student learning.

It didn't take long for us to come up with the following list:

1. Reinstate final exams—and make them worth 10% of a final grade. Students will be motivated to study when their grade is at stake.

2. Ban the use of cell phones in class unless a student's Chromebook is malfunctioning.

3. Grade more assignments on accuracy, not just completion. This distinguishes between students who have learned a lesson and those who haven't.

4. Cater lessons as much to high-achieving students as low-achieving ones. This involves making assignments more demanding for those who can handle the extra rigor.

5. Increase how many hours students spend in classrooms by reducing or eliminating activity periods, assemblies, and grade level meetings.

6. Bring back bells so students arrive to class on time. Give detention to those with three lates.

7. Understand some students aren't wired to ace the material and accept lower achievement levels for them. Not everyone is Einstein!

Our group felt we had contributed enough with seven suggestions. Then we talked shop.

"I can't believe administrators just stood over there while we worked," said Luisa, pointing to Mandy, the principal, and vice principals standing at the cafeteria's exit. "Why don't they come over to talk to us about ideas we have on how to make students work harder?"

Maria shook her head. "I think they're more interested in schmoozing."

We all laughed.

"We're the ones in the trenches," I said. "We're key to getting students to improve their reading, writing, and math skills. I hope they take seriously what we wrote on the Post-it notes."

## Characteristics of Gen Zs

**Socially defined**

Peer groups and social media platforms exert enormous influence.

**Educationally reformed**

Learning is lifelong, and that's expected.

**Digitally integrated**

Born with technology in hand.

Seamlessly integrated in daily life.

Ever-changing and updating.

**Visually engaged**

Prefer to gather knowledge by watching a video on social media.

Less likely to read an article or book.

Communicates through sharing of videos, emojis, gifs, and memes.

*Source: Pennsylvania's State System of Higher Education's "Our Generations of Students: Z and Beyond."*

Think digital in assignments, assessments, activities.

Make information graphical and bite size.

Be relevant.

Provide individualized instruction.

Use social media approaches to learning.

*Source: Dr. Vickie Cook, professor, University of Illinois.*

## Chapter Thirty

# TEACHING GEN Zs

*A* few days later, in my French 1 class, I had the chance to tell my Gen Z students about administrators' new expectations.

As usual Jason, a sturdy thirteen-year-old who resembled Dennis the Menace with his wide face and straight dirty blond hair, chattered away in English, wandering around the class as if he were networking at a cocktail party. It was halfway into the period; he had yet to start working on his worksheet on vocabulary of hobbies.

"Jason, *viens ici*," I ordered him, gesturing to come over to me.

"Huh!" he belted out. "I haven't done anything wrong. What do you want?"

"Hey, she's telling you to come over to her," said Mateo, a perfectly groomed boy with cow brown eyes.

"Jason, *prenez ton sac à dos*," I ordered him, pointing to his backpack.

The previous six weeks, I had ordered him to quiet down and work on assignments at his assigned desk. Every day he moved to a new seat, saying he just wanted to be with friends. I had allowed him this privilege thinking that maybe then he'd get some work done. But he had slacked off, preferring to chat with buddies. So much for my accommodating his social and emotional needs. That was it. He was going to sit where I told him.

"Huh, what did you say?" asked Jason, perplexed, the center of attention.

A few students blurted out he should take his backpack.

"Why do I have to?" said Jason. "I'm not doing anything wrong."

I glared at him. "You're stopping others from learning. That's not right. Everyone is going to have to work harder. At the faculty meeting, we found out how your reading and math scores on standardized tests are way down. They're below the state's average. You can't goof off anymore. Your parents are paying a lot in taxes for you to go to school here. Don't think about using your cell phone in class. It distracts you from learning. If I see a cell phone, I will confiscate it and put it in the cell phone prison."

No one uttered a word during my speech. They already knew about the hanging jewelry holder with pockets where cell phones fit perfectly.

*There was hope students would commit to learning. They had to be held accountable. Our nation depended on young people being educated.*

"Jason, you're going to work outside the classroom today. You'll use this desk," I said, pointing to one near me.

As I lugged the desk out the door, he objected with a slew of "I don't want to leave," and "Why can't I stay in the classroom?"

Other students watched the drama. One pleasant girl, who always greeted me at the beginning and end of class, smiled. She knew I would no longer take any nonsense from anyone. Other students later admitted that ever since grammar school, several students in this class had disrupted their education, and they were getting tired of it. It was the old story of a few loudmouths messing up a classroom's dynamics, making it more challenging for the majority to learn.

Without arguing, Jason exited the room.

Now students could focus on learning—though several other mischief-makers would also need disciplining.

Several times I had emailed Jason's parents about his pranks. I penned the all-important phrase that their son was behaving in a way that "created an environment not conducive to learning." He was making it difficult for others to learn—and my district took that violation seriously. Over the years I learned how to be sensitive, empathetic, factual, and kind with my words—and include at least one positive characteristic about their child. Then parents supported me, and the misbehavior often stopped. If that didn't work, I implemented a "Behavior Modification Plan." The student and I would discuss misbehavior and together we would devise a list of Dos and Don'ts and suggest a timeframe for improvement. Then we both signed this written contract. Generally students took this plan seriously, so discipline referral to administration wasn't necessary. So far Jason had avoided being placed on such a plan.

Most of the period, Jason remained outside the classroom, periodically propping open the door to peek inside to see what his classmates were doing. It was the first time I had kicked a student out of class, and frankly, I wasn't sure it was allowed. But it was effective. Other students resumed work. Just before the bell rang, I allowed Jason to return.

He grinned as he entered the room, happy to again be part of our community.

★ ★ ★

The previous fall, Jason had not been one of my students at the middle school. On the eve of school's opening, administrators had told me I'd teach an eighth grade French class. The French teacher was on paternity leave, and the district hadn't found a substitute. So every afternoon, just after lunch, I trekked over to the middle school to teach thirty thirteen-year-olds.

In September, it was tough controlling the class with many talking out of line, roughhousing, and refusing to work. I couldn't cluster their seats in groups due to Covid restrictions that required each desk to be separated by three feet. Students sat in long rows four desks deep, which made it nearly impossible to monitor every student. But I tried, learning each of their names within ten days, moving troublemakers close to my desk, and emailing parents whose kids misbehaved.

Several administrators observed my class and deemed me a competent teacher with sound pedagogical strategies. I wasn't the problem—it was kids who weren't used to the structure of school and wrongly believed they were in charge. I began to train them, and within six weeks, using lessons which kept them busy and engaged the whole period, I turned around the class. It took lots of energy—and by day's end, I was exhausted—but the effort had been worth it. They were learning and taking lessons seriously, something many of them hadn't done at home for one and a half years.

The following year, I saw how my French 1 and 2 students had benefitted from my dedication—and that of the other middle school teacher. She and I had never given up on them. Students began to realize they couldn't laze around playing video games and watching YouTube videos on their cell phones. Nor could they ignore the teacher. It was time to strive for academic excellence in the classroom, and for the district to stop coddling kids.

★ ★ ★

A month after the October faculty meeting, as I was walking to the library's Xerox machine, one of my favorite guidance counselors stopped me. She wanted to talk to me about Mikal, one of my French 3 students on medical leave. Ivy informed me Mikal had agreed to complete lessons on Educere, a provider of virtual courses for kindergarten to twelfth grade schools, for nine weeks.

"I have no idea how good the French lessons are in Educere," I said. "I picked content that aligned with what we're doing in class. But it doesn't exactly fit our curriculum."

Ivy, a forty-something-year-old wearing heels and a blazer, surveyed the corridors devoid of students, a quiet time in between periods. "Don't worry about that. Just make sure he's doing work that can be graded and posted on Genesis."

She explained how Mikal, who had already missed five weeks of school, was suffering from a medical condition and wouldn't return until late January. For long-term absences, the district and parents preferred Educere instead of assignments on Google Classroom. I wasn't quite sure why.

"Why doesn't he just drop French this year?" I asked. "I don't see how he can learn a foreign language online—particularly speaking and listening. We did that during the pandemic, and it didn't work that well."

Ivy nodded her head. "Jen, I completely agree with you. I brought up with Mikal's parents the option of dropping the class. I told them Mikal could take French 3 next year when he's a junior. His parents didn't like the idea. You know how it is around here. Parents decide what they want for their kids, and it doesn't matter what teachers and counselors say."

As a mother, I couldn't understand parents not easing a sick child's workload by having him focus only on required four-year classes such as English and PE. Once he got better, he could work on other high school graduation requirements. Evidently I thought differently than Gen Z parents.

"When he returns to school, he won't know material we covered this fall," I said. "He'll be lost. He might not pass the final exam, though I'm not sure we're having them this year."

Ivy shook her head. "I get it. But what's the point of arguing? We're not listened to. It's parents and administrators who dictate what goes on here—not us."

Just then, one of my French 2 students walked by, her head lowered, her eyes glued to the ground.

"Hi," said Ivy, greeting the student as she passed. "How are you doing today?"

"Bonjour Addy," I said. "*Ça va?*"

Addy raised her head, smiling broadly as if we were her favorite staff. "Fine. I was going to the bathroom. Here's my pass, Madame Nelson," she said, waving a piece of paper.

"No need," I said. "Good job on your dialogue."

"Thanks," she said, beaming.

"I'll see you in class later," I said.

She scooted down the corridor, her head held high. "She's such a sweet little thing," said Addy, "and obviously she has issues with self-esteem and could use our help. But we're too busy dealing with the derelicts and troublemakers that we barely have time to breathe. You know this year I'm in charge of counseling 415 students. I've met only a fraction of them."

Ivy's remarks about Addy made me think how I could try to boost her confidence, making her understand how as a diligent, humble student, she was a role model. I would make time to focus on kids who took school seriously.

During the pandemic, Ivy had talked to me about Dorian, a senior who risked not graduating if he failed French 2. Ivy was astounded that all Dorian had to do to pass French was to complete a project on farm animals. How watered down my class had become that year, but now it was time to bring back rigor. Would students support me in this challenge? Could I teach them how to be disciplined, work hard, and have a good attitude, attributes key to success in college, the workforce, and life in general? Weren't those the most important lessons I could teach them?

## Teacher Shortages

There are 16,800 public school districts and about 98,577 schools in the US.

As of July 2022, school districts had 299,000 open teaching positions.

This means each district had about 18 unfulfilled teaching positions, or three per school.

*Source: US Bureau of Labor statistics, National Center for Education Statistics, and extrapolations from this data.*

# Private Sector Offers Services to Recruit Teachers

In August 2022, ZipRecruiter, an online employment marketplace, launched a new job portal specifically for K-12 school jobs. At SchoolsJobsNearMe.org, job seekers explore various positions in public school classrooms. Schools have their job openings listed for free.

In October 2022, Handshake, an online platform for college students to find jobs, hosted a nationwide, free virtual event for undergraduate students to learn about careers in education and schools that are hiring college graduates.

In August 2022, Indeed, a global hiring platform, committed to facilitating virtual hiring fairs for educators throughout the country. Educational institutions gained access to its suite of hiring solutions. It also provided $10 million of free job advertising to support hiring events for educators.

*Source: US Department of Education and company websites.*

# Public Sector Addresses Teacher Shortages

### Apprenticeship Program

In August 2022, the Department of Labor committed to prioritizing the education sector in its next round of $100 million in apprenticeship grants. The agency provides support for states and other partners to start or expand teacher apprenticeship programs.

The program provides federal funding for on-the-job training, wages, textbooks, and childcare. Individuals receive pay while gaining teaching skills and taking courses to earn a teaching license.

Teachers' unions, state organizations, and teacher's colleges are working together to expand teacher apprenticeship programs, teaching residencies and Grow Your Own programs.

Grow Your Own programs focus on preparing community members to take teaching jobs, while teacher residency programs feature a year of student-teaching.

States with Grow Your Own programs include Tennessee, Arkansas, Colorado, Iowa, Kansas, New Hampshire, Texas, and West Virginia.

The Pathways Alliance, a coalition of public and private organizations, is creating national guidelines for registered teacher apprenticeship programs.

### American Rescue Plan Funds

In 2021, Presidents Biden's American Rescue Plan (ARP) directed $130 billion to the nation's K-12 schools. The fund allowed school districts to invest in teacher pipeline programs, increase teacher pay, and hire more professionals.

In August 2022, the Department of Education and Department of Labor urged governors and district leaders to use ARP's Elementary and Secondary School Emergency Relief funds, and $350 billion in State and Local Fiscal Recovery funds to increase teacher pay.

On average, teachers earn 33 percent less than other college-educated professionals. Adjusted for inflation, the average wages of public school teachers increased only $29 between 1996 and 2021.

### Legislation in 2022

In December 2022, Rep. Federica Wilson, D-Fla. introduced the American Teacher Act that gave incentives to states and school districts to increase the minimum K-12 teacher salary to $60,000 and provide yearly adjustments for inflation through new federal grants.

*Source: US Department of Education*

# Epilogue

As I write this in early 2023, our nation faces a crisis in education. Teachers—burned out and stressed—are leaving the profession in droves, with roughly half a million fewer teachers in our 131,000 schools. Enrollment in teacher education programs has plummeted. Most college graduates prefer majors that promise more lucrative careers. To combat this teacher shortage, districts are switching to four-day weeks, asking military veterans with teaching backgrounds to enter classrooms, and allowing college students to instruct children. Some districts are hiring virtual teachers from online education companies, while others are pulling administrators to work as substitutes and combining multiple classes in auditoriums or gymnasiums.

Will these drastic measures be enough to ensure our schools remain open with a teacher in every classroom?

For solutions, one must consider why teachers are dissatisfied with their jobs. Education experts point to pandemic-induced teacher exhaustion and low pay; some teachers sense politicians and parents have little respect for their profession. There's a rising educational culture war with districts and states restricting what teachers can say about US history, race, racism, gender, and sexual orientation. School districts banned more than 1,500 books that focus largely on race and LGBTQ issues, including the work of Nobel Prize laureate Toni Morrison. Some public schools suffer from underfunding, forcing teachers to spend their own money on resources. Many districts emphasize the importance of standardized testing.

The coronavirus pandemic led to more students with mental and behavioral health issues, and mask mandates put classrooms at the center of ideological battles. No wonder teachers are frustrated.

Fortunately, I now work in a district where parents trust and respect teachers. Administrators haven't silenced discussion on sensitive topics or censured books. The district's schools are properly funded through local taxes. Students and staff haven't objected to wearing or removing masks depending on infection rates. Resources and staff exist to support students with mental health issues, such as depression and anxiety, and learning differences.

Yet not all districts are like mine—and certainly my school isn't perfect. Due to the pandemic, different procedures had to be introduced as administrators figured out how to instruct students remotely, open schools safely, and address students' learning loss. In my school, administrators didn't have the resources to focus much on teachers' satisfaction, and the staff noticed it.

I perceive a pecking order regarding whose voices are heard. In my experience, administrators listen to parents first, then students, and finally staff. This is not a huge surprise since schools are primarily funded through local property taxes. Parents can sue a district for inequitable practices or procedures, and no district wants that liability. Next, administrators listen to students, who they worry suffer from emotional and mental health issues after sometimes experiencing years of remote learning. Administrators take seriously parents' and students' concerns and take action to solve their grievances. They should do the same with teachers.

Unfortunately, teachers' views are often considered least important. Administrators at my school appear to view teachers as expendable employees with decent salaries, and until recently, many candidates existed to fill vacant teaching positions. They mistakenly believe teachers' opinions don't matter as much—even though teachers are on the frontlines, in the classroom, seeing the impact of decisions made without their input on policies ranging from tardiness and curriculum changes to state testing mandates. Isn't it time we prioritize teachers? Our schools cannot survive another exodus of educators.

To attract more people to the profession, teaching salaries should be raised nationwide. College students must see teaching as an attractive and financially secure career. College education majors in the US make an average of only $45,000 a year, or $21.55 an hour. By comparison, in 2022, average starting salaries for computer science majors are $76,000; engineering majors, $74,000; and math and sciences major, $67,000. Educators shouldn't need a second—or third—job to make ends meet.

No wonder there's a drop in college students pursuing degrees in education. Fewer than 90,000 students were awarded education degrees in 2019, compared to the peak in the 1970s when more than 200,000 students earned this degree, according to a report from the American Association of Colleges for Teacher Education (AACTE). The report attributes the decline in teaching degrees to growing opportunities for women in other professions.

Teaching is a demanding, exhausting profession. It requires patience, energy, creativity, and dedication to keep students of all ages on track. Teachers must evolve, reinvent themselves, and embrace the latest pedagogical theory, software packages, and state education mandates. This was no clearer than during the Covid-19 pandemic when teachers taught their classes online.

Highly motivated students benefited from these interactive lessons through Zoom and Google Meet. Less disciplined students tuned school out, reluctant to work and hand in assignments without a live teacher guiding them and without in-person support from fellow students and administrators. Instead, they played video games or snoozed in their bedrooms. Administrators lowered standards; virtually all students passed classes, unrelated to their achievements.

After returning to in-person instruction, students played catch-up to master material they would otherwise have already known. In the classroom, some students experienced social anxiety, while others reveled in reconnecting with friends. Administrators encouraged teachers to closely monitor students' emotional states; students shouldn't be pushed so much they felt discouraged or depressed. I was forced to slow down my teaching, having to reduce the number of units I covered each marking period and eliminate tests that assess proficiency. I graded students on classwork, projects, and quizzes. The first year we returned to in-person teaching, administrators cancelled final exams, believing these tests would do more harm than good. I objected to my school's deteriorating academic rigor, seeing it as a disservice to young people who needed to prepare for the demands of college and the workforce. Will the following years be any better?

Administrators must renew their commitment to high standards in academic achievement, not watering down the value of a high school diploma. Our nation should listen more carefully to the opinions of teachers. Our teachers must be trusted to educate our youth; parents should show more respect and support them in this mission; and administrators should believe teachers' voices are as important as those of parents and students. By implementing these measures, we can improve our schools, and I hope, change young people's perception of the profession, so more want to enter—and stay—in it.

Looking back over fifteen years of teaching, I feel fortunate that I didn't quit after my terrible first-year experience at Northern. In addition to numerous benefits, the profession allowed me the time to raise my children, instead of leaving this role largely to a babysitter or after-care program. My three kids and I spent long summers and holidays together, my job not overshadowing my role as a mother. During their childhood they were watched over and loved, growing into the confident, kind, and successful adults they are today.

Key to my personal and professional success was the support of dozens of people who provided insight and advice into how to succeed in the classroom. Colleagues set me on the right path when I veered off. Friends emphasized how I had the personality necessary to be a good teacher. Parents supported me when their child misbehaved, and administrators guided me. My kids provided advice on how to be a cool, hip teacher. These people believed in me, and through amalgamating their advice with my own personality, I developed a teaching style truly my own. Gradually I relaxed in my classroom, confident about reaching even the toughest teens.

Over the years I changed my views about what makes great teachers. I believe they must know their subject matter, be able to discipline out-of-control teenagers, and create engaging lessons. They must treat all students fairly, and consistently enforce school rules and procedures. They should telegraph professionalism in dress, manner, and practices. They should accept the responsibilities of attending faculty meetings and professional development days.

The greatest lesson I learned is that it's okay to show students you care about them. Get to know your students. Discover their interests. Care about their progress, laugh in class with them, and listen to their joys and sorrows no matter how outrageous their opinions are. Most importantly, don't be afraid to be a Teacher with Heart.

# ABOUT THE AUTHOR

JENNIFER NELSON is a high school French teacher, writer, and personal historian. She spent the last fifteen years teaching in public and private schools; before that, she wrote for magazines and newspapers. She runs Your Stories, a writing services company, and holds undergraduate and graduate degrees from Columbia University, University of California, Berkeley and Vermont College of Fine Arts. During her spare time, she loves walking, traveling, and spending time with her partner and three grown children. She lives in Bucks County, Pennsylvania.

## SELECTED TITLES FROM SHE WRITES PRESS

She Writes Press is an independent publishing company founded to serve women writers everywhere. Visit us at www.shewritespress.com.

*Among the Maasai: A Memoir* by Juliet Cutler. $16.95, 978-1-63152-672-5. When Juliet leaves the United States to teach at the first school for Maasai girls in East Africa, she does so in the hopes that her work there will empower young women who face overwhelming odds—poverty, forced marriages, rape, and genital cutting. Working alongside local educators, Juliet is transformed by the community she finds in Tanzania and by witnessing the life-changing impact of education on her students.

*Freedom Lessons* by Eileen Harrison Sanchez. $16.95, 978-1-63152-610-7. A heartfelt, unflinching novel about the unexpected effects of school integration in 1960s Louisiana told by three very different people living in the same rural town: Colleen, an idealistic young white teacher; Frank, a black high school football player; and Evelyn, an experienced black teacher.

*How Sweet the Bitter Soup: A Memoir* by Lori Qian. $16.95, 978-1-63152-614-5. After accepting an exciting job offer—teaching at a prestigious school in China—Lori found herself in Guangzhou, China, where she fell in love with the culture and with a man from a tiny town in Hubei province. What followed was a transformative adventure—one that will inspire readers to use the bitter to make life even sweeter.

*Falling Together: How to Find Balance, Joy, and Meaningful Change When Your Life Seems to be Falling Apart* by Donna Cardillo. $16.95, 978-1-63152-077-8. A funny, big-hearted self-help memoir that tackles divorce, caregiving, burnout, major illness, fears, and low self-esteem—and explores the renewal that comes when we are able to meet these challenges with courage.

*The Buddha at My Table: How I Found Peace in Betrayal and Divorce* by Tammy Letherer. $16.95, 978-1-63152-425-7. On a Tuesday night, just before Christmas, after he had put their three children in bed, Tammy Letherer's husband shattered her world and destroyed every assumption she'd ever made about love, friendship, and faithfulness. In the aftermath of this betrayal, however, she finds unexpected blessings—and, ultimately, the path to freedom.